D0617265

The Dominion of Man

THE

The Search for

DOMINION

Ecological Responsibility

OF MAN

•

JOHN BLACK

for the University Press
Edinburgh

1970

© John Black 1970
Edinburgh University Press
22 George Square, Edinburgh
ISBN 0 85224 186 0
N. America
Aldine Publishing Company
529 S. Wabash Avenue, Chicago
Printed in the Netherlands
by Joh. Enschedé en Zonen, Haarlem

Preface

In February 1969, at the invitation of the University College London, I delivered a course of three Special University Lectures in Conservation, under the general title of 'Western World-View and the Inevitability of the Ecological Crisis'. The comments of some who heard them, and my own dissatisfaction with much of the text, decided me to revise and expand these lectures for publication as a book.

I have long been aware that there is no book I can recommend to my students of applied ecology to help them gain an historical perspective, or to show them the tacit assumptions on which their attitudes to the world are based. I hope they will find this book of mine useful, despite the unfamiliarity of much of the material to scientists, and the risks I have taken in condensing so much scholarly literature from a wide range of specialist disciplines. To make the book more easily read, I have accepted a self-denying ordinance in the matter of footnotes and have added a short selected list of references, which may serve as a 'launching-pad' for anyone wishing to pursue this subject in greater depth.

I do not think that this book could have been completed without the generous and patient encouragement I have received from many of my colleagues, either in general discussion or by their comments on the text. It seems invidious to single out a few for special mention but the debt I owe to the following is so great that it can be redeemed only in this way, and then but partially : Dr D. O. Edge, Professor R. W. Hepburn, Rev. Professor John McIntyre, Professor J. D. B. Mitchell. I owe a very great deal to my colleagues in the Department of Forestry and Natural Resources, particularly Dr C. J. Taylor, for their willingness to discuss my ideas. Needless to say, responsibility for the sins of omission or commission of which I am guilty rests squarely on my own shoulders.

Finally I want to acknowledge with especial gratitude the encouragement I have received from my friend Archie Turnbull, Secretary to the Edinburgh University Press ; and from my wife, Wendy, who created the environment in which I was able to write this book.

John Black
Professor of Natural Resources
University of Edinburgh
23 December 1969

Contents

1

The Ecological Crisis

We are living today in a society frightened by what is happening to its environment. Phrases such as 'population explosion', 'technological disaster', 'biological time-bomb', 'ecological crisis' (whatever some of them may mean) have become so widely used that they have almost lost their scare value. It seems that western civilization, with centuries of scientific knowledge and technological development to its credit, is in danger of destroying the world it set out to create. Progress, which has been defined by a twentieth century geographer as 'increasing ability to dominate the forces of nature', appears to many people to have led either to a situation in which far-reaching technical developments are initiated without adequate understanding of their ramifications, or, what is worse, to the deliberate acceptance of procedures known to be unsatisfactory simply because they are cheap or easy to implement. The result is a rapid deterioration in the quality of the human environment. No one would claim that this disillusion with the condition of western civilization is universal, but it is certainly widespread, and causes great concern, not only to individuals who happen to be sensitive to their environment, but also to governments and international organizations. Programmes for conservation, for the rational use of the resources of the biosphere or for the control of technical interference with the environment, indicate a realization that all is not well.

The branch of science which is concerned with the inter-relations of living organisms and the totality of their environment, and which is therefore involved in man's use of his world, is ecology. Ecology is a word frequently used rather loosely, but it was introduced in clear enough terms a century ago, by Haeckel. Under the General Laws of Biology, in his *History of Creation*, he wrote :

'9. The oecology of organisms, the knowledge of the sum of the relations of organisms to the surrounding outer world, to organic and inorganic conditions of existence ; the so-called "economy of nature", the correlations between all organisms living together in one and the same locality, their adaptation to their surroundings, their modification in the struggle for existence, especially the circumstances of parasitism, etc.'

Haeckel was an active propagandist in Germany for the cause of evolutionary theory, and he continued with a comment which reflected the underlying tensions of the period in which he lived :

'It is just these phenomena in "the economy of nature" which the unscientific, on a superficial consideration, are wont to regard as the wise arrangements of a Creator acting for a definite purpose, but which on a more attentive examination show themselves to be the necessary results of mechanical causes.'

If we ask why the study of ecology has failed to prevent the deterioration of the human environment, we must recognize that, during its development, it has, by and large, overlooked the relation of man to his environment, preferring to concentrate on other animals and on plants. Consequently, there are as yet few fully worked-out principles by which the impact of man on his surroundings can be assessed, so that, at a time when guidance from ecologists is being called for, it cannot be confidently offered. Nor is it possible to afford the time needed to produce the basic evidence on which advice must be based. Thus the present times offer a particular challenge to ecology, to develop a social function which can enable it to provide the scientific basis for man's control of his environment.

During the present century, two matters, among many, have caused particular disquiet. The first of these was the growing evidence that certain plant and animal species were disappearing from places where they had previously been widespread, and that many were becoming extinct. (The decline and fall of the passenger pigeon in America was a well-publicized instance of species lost through the impact of man, though it is just one of many.) The realization that many species were facing extinction gave rise to a well-organized and articulate protest movement, particularly strong among ornithologists, aimed at the preservation of threatened nature, which succeeded in awakening public consciousness of the dangers to the survival of wildlife in a technological society. The reasons which led people to protest were not always clearly understood, but a threat was recognized and, in the course of time, legislative control over some of the practices leading to extinction was secured in many parts of the world. It is often forgotten that although many species decline as a direct result of man's activities, either because they are sought after for food or similar purposes—for instance, whales in the Atlantic Ocean—or because they are competitors or predators—just as the last wolf in Scotland was reputedly killed in 1743—, the disappear-

ance of species from the face of the earth is a natural phenomenon arising out of evolutionary processes or major
changes in climate over long periods of time. (So, too, is the
appearance of species, in which man has also lent a hand.) It
was the apparently wanton elimination of species at an ac-
celerating rate that aroused protest, in societies sufficiently
endowed with resources to be able to spare some thought to
emotional and aesthetic consideration for nature.

The second and more recent source of concern has been
growing pollution of the environment. Pollution in this instance covers a wide range of matters, amongst them being
the pollution of the atmosphere by smoke and gases ; of
water by heat, sewage, or the by-products of industrial processes ; of ecological systems by radioactive fall-out, mer-
cury from seed dressings and toxic residues from pesticides
such as the chlorinated hydrocarbons ; of the human body
by barbiturates, antibiotics and even thalidomide ; of outer-
space by copper needles.

There is, of course, more to the current concern for the
environment than pollution and the need to protect threatened nature. The rapid depletion of the world's energy
resources suggests that currently available stocks of coal
and oil are unlikely to last more than a few centuries. The
possibilities of nuclear energy notwithstanding, a pious belief in the future achievements of science is not one of the
characteristics of an age which has seen too much backlash
from the application of new technologies. Changes in methods of land use in many parts of the world are likely to
result in less rather than more use being made of traditional
sources of energy such as wood and dung, and the further
development of water power involves alteration of landscapes
in remote areas increasingly sought after for solitude and
public recreation.

Underneath all these fears for the future quality of the human environment lurks the familiar spectre of rapid population growth and the attendant risk of starvation. Feeding the hungry millions is not at present a matter of scientific research and invention ; the problems are centred on political and economic aspects of world trade and the distribution of food. Unquestionably it would be technically possible to increase current food production many times over, but with present rates of population growth it is impossible to avoid the feeling that the time will surely come when the quality, if not also the quantity, of the diet of advanced western societies, let alone that of the rest of the world, must fall. Whether this time comes in one century or ten, the foreboding remains.

On further analysis, these instances of 'threatened' species and pollution are seen to be by-products of human intervention in natural processes with the object of increasing the yield of products of resource systems. These interventions aim at replacing natural by artificial ecosystems, and involve a progressive simplification of the biological environment. As the population : resource ratio narrows, there is less and less room for anything which competes with man for the ecological raw materials ; plants and animals not providing economic returns are eliminated ; mixed woodlands are replaced by monocultures of trees or farm crops ; natural pastures of great floristic diversity give way to ultra-simple swards of, perhaps, one or two species only ; hedges are removed ; ignorance, stupidity or greed lead to large tracts of land being ruined by inappropriate cropping ; populations of wild ungulates are replaced by poorly adapted domestic cattle ; disturbance of catchment areas is followed by flooding. As technological complexity increases, there are new reasons for concern when, to take just two examples, oil is discharged in large quantities from a wrecked tanker and the remedial applications of detergent cause more damage to the coastal beaches than did the oil, or insecticide poisons 250 miles of the river Rhine, dislocating traffic, killing the fish and endangering water supplies. Although the opposition to ecological simplification was based initially on emotional or aesthetic grounds, it has become increasingly clear that a strong case can be made out on economic and scientific criteria as well.

Progressive simplification of ecosystems is inevitable if increasing food production is required. It is widely accepted that stability, diversity and productivity in ecosystems are associated in such a way that as productivity of one component species increases, stability and diversity are reduced. Hence simplification carries with it the risk of disruption, since the ecological homeostasis (that is, the ability of an ecosystem to resist change, to return to equilibrium after disturbance—for instance, to recover from excessive grazing ; to react to invasion by pest or disease species, by 'containing' the invaders ; to regrow after fire, flooding or windblow—) is lost with simplification.

More dangerous, though, than excessive simplification are badly chosen land use practices, such as growing crops where rainfall is insufficient or where the soil surface is left exposed to wind or storm damage, with the resultant erosion typified by the Dust Bowl of the United States between the wars. The Scottish Highlands provide an example of a man-made wet desert ; a long history of erosion resulting from deforestation and sheep farming have led to ecological stagnation. There are not many clear demonstrations of the progressive effects of cultivation over long periods of time, but recent evidence from soil cores in a small lake near Rome suggests that there was a sudden increase in sedimentation about 2,000 years ago, at the time when intensive cultivation began in the surrounding countryside following the construction of a new road. The rates of erosion calculated from the sedimentation were about 3 cm/1,000 years before cultivation began, and 30 cm thereafter—a tenfold increase in an area where, despite the vulnerability of the 'mediterranean' climate, an agricultural ecology might be expected to have been satisfactory and stable.

One of the most worrying features of the present attempts to change the environment is the way in which new processes are all too often introduced without adequate knowledge of their possible long-term effects. Examples are not hard to find : the use of certain pesticides was widely adopted before it was realized that they are progressively concentrated along food-chains, reaching lethal levels in 'terminal' species, and that the dosage is cumulative ; synthetic detergents when first introduced led to appalling problems of disposal through normal sewage processes ; the drug thalidomide was widely prescribed as a tranquillizer before it was associated with malformations of the human foetus. Sometimes the results of technical processes can be predicted, but are overlooked on grounds of ignorance, expediency, or the lack of an economically attractive alternative. Examples of this include the effect of sewage effluent on a river system ; the discharge of heated water from cooling plants on the fish population downstream ; the disposal of industrial waste products including, in one case, mothproofing insecticides into inland waters ; or the construction of spoil heaps from a coalmine on a geologically unsuitable hillside.

It is perhaps unreasonable to lay much blame on those who initiate new processes, since the possible side effects may be so remote from experience that they are not checked, even if means were available of doing so. It is important to retain a sense of proportion ; no doubt if cigarette smoking were to be introduced for the first time today, the possibility of carcinogenic effects might be investigated, and the world spared a dangerous and dirty practice. Perhaps the gastro-intestinal side effects of that well-known household standby, the humble aspirin, would nowadays prevent its first appearance on the market. Nevertheless, the rapidly increasing number of new techniques involves an ever-increasing risk of the introduction of methods having dangerous but unsuspected side effects. Even if a higher proportion of potentially toxic processes are detected by improved methods of examination, the absolute number of instances escaping detection is still likely to increase, and public concern to grow.

One familiar reaction to the present situation is to put all the blame for the ills of the world on to science and techno-logy, but this is sheer evasion. It is the uses to which science and technology are put, and the attitudes and changes they engender, which must be examined if we are to understand how it has come about that, with widespread and formidable techniques at our disposal, the environment in which we live—and which we have very largely shaped—is not to our liking.

We are apt to underestimate the extent to which man has altered the environment of the earth. In the early days of human evolution, man would have fitted easily into his environment, being a natural and integral component of the ecosystem of which he was a part. Presumably he made no more impact on his surroundings than any other similar animal species, but his wide environmental tolerance, through physiological adaptability to a variety of external conditions and a range of diets, enabled him to spread over a large part of the globe. With the development of tools, first for hunting and later for agriculture, his ability to change his surroundings increased, and he began to see himself as in some way apart from the ecosystem on which he depended. Probably the most powerful, as well as one of the earliest, tools with which man interfered with his environment was fire. As an adjunct to hunting, its effect on altering the vegetation was probably more important than its role in increasing the kill of prey, and, even without hunting, 'escapes' from camp fires, if sufficiently frequent, may have changed the vegetation drastically enough to eliminate elements of the local fauna. It has recently been suggested that about 10,000 years ago, towards the end of the Quarternary period, the lighting of fires by Australian aborigines was in this way responsible for the extinction of some early marsupials. The use of fire to remove forest vegetation and to maintain savanna grasslands in its place is known to be of long standing, so that at a time when man's predatory ability was still rudimentary, and the possibility of his hunting having a critical effect on his prey thus remote, his use of fire would by itself account for major changes in vegetation and its associated animal species. With the development of settled agriculture, the domestication of plants and animals, and the use of such relatively sophisticated techniques as irrigation under semi-arid conditions, the rate and extent of technical interference with the natural ecosystem increased, until the stage has been reached when it would be hard to find any part of the world which has not been transformed by human activity. Even the penguins of Antarctica now carry residues of DDT in their tissues.

The deterioration in the quality of the environment obviously began a long time ago, and the effects of pollution, to take one criterion only, have been commented on for centuries. Stow, in his *Survey of London*, refers to a complaint that was laid before King Edward I in 1307 :

> 'that whereas in times past the course of water, running at London under Oldbourne Bridge and Fleet Bridge into the Thames, had been of such breadth and depth, that 10 or 12 ships' navies at once, with merchandise, were wont to come to the foresaid bridge of Fleet, and some of them to Oldbourne Bridge : now the same course, by filth of the tanners and such others, was sore decayed ; also by raising of wharfs ; but especially, by a diversion of the water made by them of the new Temple for their mills... and divers other impediments, so as the said ships could not enter as they were wont, and as they ought'.

London has also long been known for its foul atmosphere. When Thomas Parr, said to be 152 years old, was called to London in 1635, he promptly died ; an autopsy was performed by William Harvey who diagnosed a 'peripneumony', the chief cause of which was said to be the change of air, Parr having been exposed to smoke pollution after a lifetime spent in air of perfect clarity. John Evelyn, the diarist, described in 1661 that 'Hellish and dismall Cloud of SEA-COALE', 'perpetually imminent' over London, which was

> 'so universally mixed with the otherwise wholesome and excellent *Aer*, that her *Inhabitants* breathe nothing but an impure and thick Mist, accompanied with a fuliginous and filthy vapour, which renders them obnoxious to a thousand inconveniences, corrupting the *Lungs* and disordering the entire habit of their Bodies ; so that *Catharrs, Phthisicks, Coughs*, and *Consumptions*, rage more in this one City, than in the whole Earth besides'.

Evidently pollution is no new problem, but the current wave of protest can be accounted for in terms of several factors : firstly, pollution has become much more widespread and is increasing rapidly with the growth of industrialization and advanced agricultural technology ; secondly, sewage is discharged into the sea via the river system instead of being spread over the land as manure, a change which has not yet achieved appropriate legislative or administrative control, either at national or international levels ; thirdly, greater mobility and opportunities for leisure enable more people to visit and inspect the countryside. It may also be that an explicit concern for the quality of living is a characteristic of an affluent, leisured society. In poorer, less advanced, societies, survival rather than enjoyment becomes paramount, and there is more temptation to sacrifice long-term interests for short-term necessity.

To the ordinary man or woman, the main cause for concern is possibly not the evidence, widespread though it may be, of the pollution of the air and water, the elimination of visual beauty by an increasing monotony of landscape and ugly rural development, the disappearance of many forms of wildlife such as the flowers of roadside verges or the fish of the streams, but an underlying uneasiness that new techniques are being used without a proper appreciation of what they may bring in their train. There is in addition the familiar feeling of frustration and resignation born out of the futility of trying to retain a measure of control over high-level and far-reaching decisions which, often through a failure of communication, seem arbitrary and unreasonable. Since the anticipated growth of world population will inevitably involve increased pressure on the world's resources, the present trends must be expected to continue, and the situation to get worse. Many people in the advanced countries of western civilization are coming to the view that the application of modern technology to the countryside is

creating conditions in which they would not enjoy living ;
they sense that the point of no return may already have
been passed. The essence of the 'ecological crisis' is not that
we are ruining our environment ; it is that by ruining our
environment we are imperilling our own future. I shall have
more to say about the use of the word 'crisis' in this connection in the last chapter of this book.

Other civilizations have faced similar situations but for
obvious reasons did not designate them 'ecological crises'.
The Moa civilization of New Zealand is an interesting
example of a narrowly-based resource system in which a
wide range of the animal species on which it depended were
hunted out of existence. The New Zealand flora had evolved
in the absence of terrestrial mammals and the heavy flight-
less Moa species occupied the niche subsequently held by
grazing animals in the later European period. A density of
750–800 birds per acre has been estimated for the Canter-
bury plains. The Polynesian peoples who arrived about
1,200 years ago instituted a hunting, fowling and fishing
economy, in which the Moa was the most important provid-
er of meat, skin, feathers, bones, and eggs, the last named
being used both for food and for water containers. Fire was
used in hunting and to clear the forest vegetation, and after
600 years or so a number of bird species, including swans,
eagles and Moas had all become extinct, though some species
survived in Southland till the seventeenth century. This
change in the resources available is reflected in the increasing proportion of fishbones in the middens. Eventually
the Moa civilization gave way before an agricultural people
from the North Island, who had a strongly conservationist
attitude to plant and animal resources, and the vegetation
revived. From an ecological viewpoint, there would have
been a critical period when the increasing difficulty of

obtaining enough Moas indicated inadequate recruitment of young birds into the population so that a decline in the number of adults available for hunting was inevitable. Perhaps the change to a predominately fish diet happened so slowly that people were not aware of it, but traditional tribal memories are usually said to be long, and it is improbable that such major changes in the environment would have gone unnoticed. It would be interesting to know what these changes were ascribed to, if indeed they were noticed.

Similarly, the decline of the great Babylonian irrigated grain civilization has been put down to increasing soil salinization resulting from imperfect drainage, perhaps accompanied by changes in the rainfall regime. There was presumably a time when yields were declining, more and more unsuitable areas were being pressed into cultivation, irrigation channels were needing reconstruction and extension, while the demands of the cities were increasing ; an ecological crisis within today's meaning would have been recognized when it was realized that the limits of production had been reached and the technology of the civilization stretched to breaking point.

The notion that the world was in decline is, of course, a very old one in Western civilization. In the first century B C, Lucretius (*De Rerum Natura,* Book II) complained of the declining fertility of the earth and the increasing difficulty of wresting a living from it. The husbandman 'does not realize' he writes 'that everything is gradually decaying and nearing its end, worn out by old age'. Lucretius's exposition of the Epicurean viewpoint was answered in no uncertain terms by the writers on Roman agriculture. Columella opened his 12-book treatise *De Re Rustica* with a refutation of the view that 'the soil was worn out and exhausted by the over-production of earlier days and can no longer furnish

sustenance to mortals with its old-time benevolence'. It was
wrong to think that the earth had grown old in the same way
as a man might grow old, he continued ; misfortunes come
upon us because of our own fault, 'for the matter of husbandry, which all the best of our ancestors had treated with
the best of care, we have delivered over to all the worst of
our slaves, as if to a hangman for punishment'.

Nevertheless, the idea of the earth growing old, and declining in productivity, retained a firm grip on European
consciousness, reaching a climax in the first part of the
seventeenth century. 'The whole earth is hastening to her
last declination', wrote Fulke Greville, and it is probable
that at the back of people's minds was the long-standing
theological view that the Fall of Man was accompanied by
the Fall of all the rest of Nature. The words of the 102nd
Psalm were not forgotten :

'Of old hast thou laid the foundation of the earth : and the
heavens are the work of thy hands.

They shall perish, but thou shalt endure : yea, all of them
shall wax old like a garment ; as a vesture shalt thou
change them, and they shall be changed :

But thou art the same, and thy years shall have no end.'

The arguments over the decay of the world are best exem-
plified in the famous controversy between Goodman (*The
Fall of Man, or the Corruption of Nature Proved by the
Light of our Natural Reason,* 1616) and Hakewill (*An
Apologie of the Power and Providence of God in the
Government of the World,* 1627). Goodman listed a number
of phenomena from which he adduced the decline and decay
of nature—the infertility of the soil, the hostility of animals
to man, nature's production of low and repellent forms of
life rather than noble creatures, man's misery, fragility and
ill-health, and the inclemency of the seasons. Many of these

could easily be refuted by Hakewill as mis-reading of the evidence, but the supposed signs of decay are less significant in themselves than in the way they draw attention to different philosophical approaches.

This controversy, and the circumstances leading up to it, have been exhaustively examined by Victor Harris in his book *All Coherence Gone* so that the best way of discussing it here is to summarize his conclusions. He points out that four basic arguments were involved, 'the arguments from the purpose of creation, from the natural processes by which the world is corrupted, from the necessary and the natural destruction of the world and, finally, from the analogy between microcosm and macrocosm'.

On the first point, Goodman argued that the decay of the world turned man to the contemplation of God, to His greater glory, while Hakewill believed that a stable world better reflected the glory of God ; they were agreed in their desire to uphold divine providence. On the second, Goodman held that the tendency of the world to decay was held in check before the Fall, after which disruptive forces operated through contrary motions to bring it about ; Hakewill denied that this could cause a permanent decay. On the third point, Goodman's view was that the decay must lead to the end of the world, Hakewill's, that the end of the world, like its beginning, must come from supernatural action. On the fourth and crucial point, there is complete disagreement. Goodman held that as the world was created for man, its decay can be inferred by analogy from the senescence and death of the individual man ; Hakewill could not accept this analogy. Once it was understood that the world was not created for man alone, the analogy disappeared.

Thus, from a number of factors—physical signs and theological argument—there came about a concept of the decay and degradation of the natural environment, and a sense of the nearness of the end of the world which is paralleled, at least in outline, in today's concern over ecological disequilibria. Nevertheless, there are important differences ; while Lucretius and Goodman both drew attention to the state of the world as they saw it, neither of them seemed ready to ascribe it (as Columella did) to human activity, and there was no realization that a decline could be arrested only by a reconsideration of the application of technical processes. The difference between the seventeenth and twentieth century protests at the deterioration of the natural environment lies in this fundamental change in attitude. Even today we find experienced ecologists describing African soils as 'old and senile' as if the argument of the world's decay is still drawn from the 'microcosm' analogy, but the twentieth century is all too well aware that the problem is man-made and must be solved by man.

Since the present position has been brought about by the application of science and technology to ecological processes, the remedy is widely thought to be more science, more technology. This reliance on the application of technical control of nature is a fundamental, even a unique aspect of western civilization, so much so that it is usually taken for granted. Modern science is essentially a 'western' phenomenon, though it has taken over many elements from other cultures, Chinese, Greek and Arabic in particular, and its peculiarly western aspect is the manipulative way in which science and technology are used to alter the environment (in its widest sense) for the benefit of mankind. From Europe and North America it has spread all over the world, being held out everywhere as a panacea. It has been taken up by members of other cultures with little regard to their outlook or philosophies of nature, with the attendant stresses and strains of readjustment. This emulation of the materialistic standards of western civilization is understandable enough in developing countries, but it is not always sufficiently realized that science is only one manifestation of the western outlook, and has itself developed within a nexus of developing beliefs and ideas. Attemps to graft an attitude of technical control of nature onto a non-western philosophy implies either the eventual acceptance of a totally western way of life, or else a gradual and probably painful period of adaptation and compromise. The dominance of western culture in the world is such that the export of western science is accepted as the only way of development, an attitude implicitly accepted by international agencies in their attempts to raise living standards in the poorer countries. In this way all parts of the world are set on the road leading to development through technological progress, whether this is compatible with the rest of their outlook or not. Whatever the native scientific achievements of other cultures may have been or may be, the use of science to dominate the forces of nature is a fundamental and long-held component of western civilization, and its apparent success hitherto has led to its world-wide adoption.

The recognition that the use of science to control natural processes has brought the western world to a point when it is beginning to doubt its future survival thus appears to be a criticism of the way in which scientific knowledge has been used in development. It suggests that ecological breakdown need not have occurred, had the scientific abilities of western civilization been used in different directions, or used more wisely. Emphasis on the accumulation of scientific knowledge or even the will to use it to improve the conditions under which man was living do not however make this situation inevitable. Why then has it come? The reason is to be found not in science or technology alone, but in the whole complex of ideas on which western civilization is based. Given certain assumptions of an ideational nature, an ecological breakdown was bound to occur sooner or later. That it should be the middle of the twentieth century when it is recognized is not of itself important. At some time it would have come, depending on the rate and direction of technical development, the increase in world population and the changing attitude of man to the rest of nature. It does not follow that this is the last, let alone the only period of ecological disruption through which western civilization must pass ; with appropriate advances in technology, this one may be averted, though it is not easy at the moment to see how this might come about. Given the underlying attitudes, a similar position will sooner or later be reached again. Perhaps ecological breakdown will recur until either the environment deteriorates faster than the increases in technology needed to restore it, or man reconsiders his basic attitudes to life, and adjusts his view of his place in the world accordingly. These alternatives may seem pessimistic ; the optimistic alternative—that the present tail-chasing relationship between increasing pressure on the world's natural resources and technological advances can be sustained—seems to have little possibility in the very long term, whatever its scope in the next few decades or even centuries may be.

2

The Western World-View

It is a commonplace of contemporary thinking that the
problems of the world are those of underdevelopment, and
that they can be solved only by a measure of further development, leading to a vicious circle in which more, or more
advanced, technology only serves to intensify the existing
situation. This is so firm a part of our approach to man's
place on the earth that it comes as rather a shock to find
advocates of a totally different view, that the really serious
and intractable problems of the world today are those of
over development, not *under* development. This is the attitude taken by Nasr, a philosopher and historian of science of
the Muslim faith, in his book *The Encounter of Man and
Nature*. He argues that western civilization, in seeking to
impose ever-increasing control of natural processes, has lost
'the sense of the spiritual significance of nature'. Nature has
become merely something to be exploited, so much so that
the position has now been reached when the future of man
on the earth is imperilled. In acting as a critic of the West,
Nasr emphasises that the basic attitudes of western civilization may not be the most appropriate on which to base the
future development of the world's resources, and he

prompts us to question the way in which we seek to use our scientific knowledge and technical abilities. 'Although science is legitimate in itself', he writes, 'the role and function of science and its application have become illegitimate and even dangerous because of the lack of a higher form of knowledge into which science could be integrated and the destruction of the sacred and spiritual value of nature.'

The domination of nature by extreme technical control as the true end of man is essentially a European-American preoccupation, and is in sharp contrast to Nasr's plea for the elaboration of a metaphysical doctrine which would re-establish man's place in nature, perhaps substituting *harmony with nature* for *dominion over nature* as the guiding principle. Are there then some features in the philosophies underlying the development of western civilization which have encouraged the uncompromising treatment of the natural environment and its resources, which in its turn has led to our present concern over ecological stability? If, indeed, there are such special features, how did they arise, what circumstances accompanied their development, and what do they imply for the future?

To answer these questions, we need to understand how western man thinks about his environment ; what is his attitude to his surroundings—the cosmos, known and unknown, and the way in which it came into being ; his immediate problems of birth, life and death ; his relation to other people and, equally important, to the rest of animate and inanimate nature ; his relation to the whole of his external world—in other words, his place 'in the scheme of things'. There is no really satisfactory English word for this sense of looking out of oneself at the rest of the world, though in German there is the perfectly adequate word 'Weltanschauung'. It is not easy to find an adequate translation of this compound word, but of the various possibilities, 'world-view' seems to come closest. One word which certainly will not do is 'religion', since it is, for us, too much confused with ecclesiolatry and the observance of certain forms of worship to convey the necessary meaning ; the widespread separation of man's spiritual concepts from the social and economic considerations of everyday life merely emphasizes its unsuitability.

A world-view must clearly comprise many different strands of opinion, but in its totality it has to provide the individual with a means of coming to terms with the realities of his world or, at least, to interpret these realities in a way which can be meaningful to him, within the whole context of his beliefs. Some of the components of a world-view must be directed towards informing the individual how he should act in relation to his world, such as the way in which, and the extent to which, he can organize his surroundings. Others will seek to establish a basis for conduct and will involve the significance placed on the rest of nature, animal, vegetable or mineral, as well as on human life. Other strands of thought will seek to provide some explanation of the origin of the world and of man. A world-view will be the more satisfactory, the better it is able to reconcile the individual with the various components of his environment, even if this involves an interpretation of these components which is not strictly in accordance with reality.

The most important aspects of our own, western world-view which contribute in this way may be listed as follows, though the enumeration is not intended to suggest a grading in importance :

(1) A conviction that man's role on earth is to exploit the rest of nature to his own advantage,

(2) An expectation of continuing population expansion,

(3) A belief in progress and history, with an underlying
   linear concept of time,

(4) A concern for posterity.

These ideas are present to a greater or lesser degree, I
believe, in the world-view of the vast majority of the people
in western civilization, though not, perhaps, in the precise
way in which they have now been formulated, and they are
obviously highly inter-correlated. They are held, needless to
say, by people who are intellectually incapable of formu-
lating them for themselves ; they have permeated into the
instinctive inheritance of society, being passed from generation to generation by example, by instruction and as
components of current mythology. Consequently, in many
ways they are apt to defy analysis, in that many people hold
them without being able to explain them in meaningful
terms when called upon to do so. Even highly intelligent
and articulate people adhere to attitudes towards the surrounding world which they have never consciously moulded
or debated within themselves, but which they have accepted
as they stand and have taken for granted. Frequently they
are quite unaware of them. Indeed, many of our most
deeply-seated attitudes to life *are* unconsidered. Baillie,
writing about the belief in progress, summed it up like this :

'It is essentially a philosophy of life ; and like all philosophies of life, it does duty for a religion ; and like all
philosophies and all religions, its deepest root is in certain
a priori presuppositions which may receive welcome
support from experience *a posteriori,* or alternatively be
troubled by the lack of it, but are themselves beyond the
reach of the discursive understanding.'

Many, perhaps most, people can be forgiven for not
devoting the necessary time and effort to elaborating their
own world-view, or, indeed, to questioning their received

modes of thinking. It is, in any case, hard for an individual to separate his own world-view from the one generally accepted by the society of which he is a member. As long as he is able to interpret the outside world in a consistent and satisfying manner, without too many jarring conflicts, there may be little need for him to consider his own attitudes.

The components of western world-view which have been mentioned as relevant, within the totality of beliefs, to the relationship of man to his immediate environment, even if they have been reduced here to undeserved simplicity, are ideas of great and lasting importance. Such ideas grow slowly from unimagined beginnings, becoming accepted gradually, eventually perhaps becoming codified. For long periods they may exist only in the oral traditions of a culture and over the course of historical time they may be fused, discarded or regrouped in response to changes in the external conditions of the society or in the internal conditions brought about by the development of the society itself. No better study of the changes in attitude to the world can be recommended than C. S. Lewis' *The Discarded Image*, an absorbing and highly relevant examination of the medieval model of the universe, its influence and its breakdown. Amongst other things, Lewis shows how important it is for a society to possess a satisfying and consistent understanding of its world, even though this may be suspected or even known not to be entirely 'true'. When the time comes, as come it must, when the accepted model is openly admitted to be lacking in some particulars, it has to be rejected. A new one emerges to take its place, and the necessary evidential building-blocks will be found to hand, ready to be used to construct a new image.

If we wish to understand our present attitudes to the world outside us, we need to trace our views back to their

origins in the early intellectual development of our culture,
and to follow the ways in which they varied with the passage
of time, remembering that ideas brought into a world-view
from any particular source persist even when the source
itself is no longer important or has been generally forgotten.
Ideas once assimilated acquire a momentum independent of
the framework in which they initially appeared, and their
dependence on and association with other concepts become
blurred or overlooked, even though they may be unable to
stand on their own feet as a result. For instance, western
world-view incorporates many fundamental concepts derived from Judeo-Christian sources ; if Christianity is no
longer universally accepted as a faith, many of the ideas
based on it nevertheless remain. Much of the restlessness of
the contemporary western world is the result of the elimination of those aspects of our world-view *directly* dependent
upon religion, such as the concept of salvation or a belief in
the life after death, and the lack of suitable and satisfying
alternatives to take their place.

Many different elements have combined to form the
western world-view, assimilated from different sources and
at different times. Of these various elements, three are of
outstanding importance : Greek philosophy and intellectual
method ; Hebrew theology and its reinterpretation in Christianity ; Roman concepts of law and organization. Other
influences, such as Chinese or Arabic science, have also
provided growing points in the development of western
thought. Of all these different sources, the one most relevant
to our attitudes towards the natural environment, its use
and its abuse, is that one which we can most conveniently
describe as 'Judeo-Christianity'. Much of this book is devoted to a study of the way in which this has coloured the
development of our own thinking, and inevitably involves

us in the creation legends enshrined in the Book of Genesis. Hence it is important to be quite clear about this particular aspect of our cultural inheritance.

It is now generally accepted that the Book of Genesis, as we know it, was edited from a number of older texts. This is not to suggest that a selection of earlier material had not previously been brought together ; there is some evidence that a text had been in existence for several centuries before the final redaction, during which time the final form was taking shape. The original texts which were gradually fused together to provide the edited version were of much greater antiquity, in all probability stretching back into the oral traditions of the people. Over these centuries, a number of changes were incorporated to bring the old texts into closer conformity with reality. In a compilation of this nature, it is difficult, if not impossible, to distinguish between the different levels of conceptual organization we can designate as myth, saga, and history. There seems to be fairly general agreement among Old Testament scholars that from the time of David onwards we are increasingly concerned with historical truth, but although archaeological research is increasingly confirming the earlier historical components of the Old Testament, it is by no means clear where the line should be drawn between history and non-history. For our purposes we should wish to treat as history matters of fact concerning the existence of named individuals who lived at a given point of time. Similarly, we would classify, as saga, stories of people who may or may not have existed at some time or other, stories which have become inflated or distorted to point a moral, or perhaps to hold out some characteristic or characteristics of personal conduct deemed worthy of emulation, or perhaps some which would be best avoided. Depending on the purpose of the particular exami-

nation, history may have to be separated from saga, and
both from myth. For the establishment of the origin of our
attitudes to the rest of nature, and the associated components of our world-view, neither history nor saga is likely to
be particularly valuable, except inasmuch as they serve to
illustrate or illuminate the changing significance placed on
certain concepts and opinions as society developed. We
must also recognize that one of the aims of the editors of the
Book of Genesis was to place the traditional material in a
historical context, with the intention of demonstrating the
gradual development of the Hebrew nation from the creation onwards. The material is accordingly presented in
such a way as to reveal the fulfilment of the Divine Purpose
in the destiny of a chosen people. This, in turn, presupposes
the organization of mythical and legendary material in a
temporal sequence emphasizing the evolution of Hebrew
society, and since significant attitudes to the external world
are most likely to be developed initially at the mythological
level, it is necessary to enquire in a little more detail into the
function of myth and, in particular, into the mythogony of
Genesis.

Firstly, the nature of mythical thought should be clearly
understood. There are two basic approaches to myth; one is
to regard it as a collection of symbols which, when brought
together into something akin to a fairy story, provide an
apparent explanation of phenomena for which no rational
explanation is otherwise forthcoming. The myth tells a story,
interesting and perhaps satisfying on its face value alone, but
of significance to an objective observer when examined as an
example of the problems faced by a society in coming to
terms with the realities of its environment. The second view
of myth is to see it as united to the social patterns of the society, tied to an explanation of the origin and perpetuation of

social activities, and incapable of existing in the absence of this link with function. (Lévi-Strauss' *'structural analysis'* depends on a detailed examination of all the components of a myth, in all the various forms in which it exists, in order to present the structure as a statistical pattern of the various symbols contained within it, and is related to the first, or symbolic view). The purpose of myth is thus the elaboration of a model by which contradictions in the physical or intellectual environment may be avoided, and an important aspect is the way in which these contradictions are avoided or 'mediated' by the accumulation of similar myths which operate together within the whole framework of a society's beliefs, the effect of each constituent story being to reinforce the feeling of opacity which surrounds unpleasant and contradictory situations, real or imagined. Reiteration of information in different versions increases confidence in the message to be 'got across', and operates towards the elimination of confusions arising from misreadings or misinterpretations, or what the engineer would describe as 'background noise'. It is not then surprising to find in the Book of Genesis several strands of narrative, in different versions, which seem to tell the same story, or to put across the same message, albeit in slightly different ways.

It follows from this that the same mythical material can carry a number of different patterns, or interpretations, depending on the standpoint of the observer and his views on the place of myth in culture, and, perhaps, his judgment of what are the significant contradictions which require explanation or resolution. This point was very neatly put by Mary Douglas in these terms : 'Compare St Augustine, Simone Weil (1950) and Edmund Leach (1962) on the Biblical story of Noah drunk in the vineyard : for one the drunken, naked Noah is Christ humiliated ; for the other he is the dionysian mysteries too austerely rejected by the Jewish priesthood, and for the last the tale is a trite lesson about Hebrew sexual morality'. Similarly, an ecologist turning his attention to the Judeo-Christian creation legends will seek—and will perhaps find—evidence relating to his own particular purposes. Hence the examination of myth has to be handled with transparent intellectual honesty. It is also especially important to rid the mind of such notions as 'myths are only fairy-stories' or 'myths have only to do with ancient Greek gods or heroes' and to remember that our own thinking relies heavily on myth (using the word always in the scholarly sense) in the way we face up to—or avoid—the realities of life.

There is, of course, a long tradition of theological and philosophical study of the mythological content of the Old Testament, which Childs has usefully summarized for the non-specialist. He draws attention to the way in which the understanding of world order in terms of mythology has created tensions when the 'mythical' explanation comes into conflict with Old Testament concepts of reality, and how the process of assimilation proceeded at different rates and to different extents. In the early parts of the Book of Genesis we have before us a document which reflects the way the original mythical material was hammered into theological shape, and reflects, too, a long period of gestation in which the various components of the Hebraic world-view fell into place. Once this period of gestation had been accomplished, the basic attitudes to the world were fixed, and they remained fixed, almost without change, until comparatively recently. Some of them, including those most important for an understanding of modern man's attitude to nature, and hence of the ecological crisis with which he is now faced, remain unchanged today.

3

Dominion over Nature

The relationship in western civilization between man and his environment has gradually changed over evolutionary time from a condition of integration within nature to one of domination from without nature ; other civilizations have not necessarily accepted the separation of man from the rest of nature to the same extent. In the earliest times, man or his hominid antecedents had neither the ability nor, we may suspect, the desire to change his surroundings. He formed part of the natural ecosystem, as did other mammalian species, at secondary and tertiary trophic levels, affecting the cycling of energy, nutrients and water in much the same way. Gradually this situation changed, with the development of the necessary techniques for fishing, hunting, and, eventually, the domestication of plants and animals, to the position of control of nature which is accepted, often unthinkingly, as the proper role of man on earth today.

In this sequence of the gradual independence of man from his place in the natural ecosystem there are clearly two separate processes, no matter how intricately they may have been cross-related. The first of these two processes is the development of the technical ability to modify the environment, to impose some different functional pattern upon it, and eventually to transform it. The second process is the development of the desire to do this, to intervene purposefully in natural processes for the benefit of the human race. Over one hundred years ago, the pioneer social philosopher, Auguste Comte, wrote—'Civilization consists, strictly speaking, on the one hand, in the development of the human mind, on the other, in the result of this, namely, the increasing power of Man over Nature.' He evidently believed that power over nature was derived from the use of the intelligence, and implied that the means of controlling nature followed the desire to do so, and the application of man's inventiveness to the development of the necessary techniques. His words underlie the attitude of the nineteenth and early twentieth century in Europe to the rest of the world ; progress meant the domination of nature, and only by increasing this domination could the evils and short-comings of life on earth be removed. Today we are perhaps much less confident of the advantages of power over nature, now that the results of power without responsibility are all too obvious everywhere. This is one of the most important reasons for the general swing away from science and technology, and towards a search for deeper meanings in life, which is so marked a feature of the present day. Few would question the value of science as an intellectual discipline : it is the way in which science has been used which is in question.

It will probably never be possible to separate entirely the *ability* and the *desire* to increase control over nature as they developed in the early stages of biological and social evolution of man, since ability and desire must surely have marched hand-in-hand. Once a stage had been reached in which purposeful interference could be recognized, a conscious attitude to nature would have been elaborated. Sooner or later, man would have been presented with the necessity of choosing between alternative methods of using techniques already available, or with deciding what intensity of intervention was required in any particular set of conditions. In the course of time came the knowledge that biological resources can all too easily be over-exploited, leading to a decrease, or even a cessation, of production. Such knowledge, the accumulated fruits of bitter experience, would be reflected in symbolic and other forms in the oral traditions of the society, and a mythological superstructure elaborated to cover not only man's conscious attitude to nature but also the ways in which his ability to interfere with natural processes was to be circumscribed in the interests of long-term security.

There is interesting evidence of the developing attitude of western man to his environment in the Book of Genesis, but before turning to the important sections of the text, some further discussion of this Book is necessary. There are, as is well known, two separate narratives intertwined in Genesis ; one, known as 'J', from the author's use of 'Jahweh', as the name of God, was probably written down in the ninth or tenth century BC, codifying an ancient tradition of beliefs. The other version, 'P', or 'Priestly', also reflects a long, but different, tradition. It was not written down until the sixth or fifth century BC, after the Hebrew people had returned from exile in Babylon, and the life of the people was being reorganized under strong religious leadership. The redaction of these two sources into the Book of Genesis as we know it occurred later still. The realization that two distinct—and often contradictory—versions of the same stories exist side by side in the creation stories of Genesis explains some of the obvious discrepancies and confusions in the text, almost every verse of which is, in any case, fraught with exegetical difficulty. The lay reader is often at a loss to know where to turn in the mass of theological commentary which is available, but a simple explanatory volume such as Driver's or Richardson's is a valuable stand-by. It is less easy to understand why the two versions were not combined into one 'accepted' version, as was attempted—not entirely successfully—when the editors reached the story of the Flood.

In all quotations from Genesis, and from other books of the Bible, I shall use the Authorized Version of 1611, King James' Bible. Obviously, any translation chosen loses some of the sense of the original meaning, and on balance I think it is better to use the most familiar and, to me, the most beautiful and expressive of the many versions available, re-examining certain words and phrases where subsequent scholarship has revealed the need for re-interpretation, or where the precise meaning of an English word has changed over the last 400 or so years.

In using Genesis for the present purpose it is important to eliminate the explanatory material accumulated around the original text by subsequent commentators. The process of augmenting the original version began as early as the 'Book of Enoch' of the second century BC, and was carried forward by Philo and Josephus, by the Patristic writers, by the medieval scholars and theologians and on to the great commentators of the Renaissance. What they added helps us to realize how the ideas first put forward in Genesis were developed and understood over the progress of history, but what is required for the moment is the best possible indication of western man's early thoughts on the subject.

Chapter 1, verses 26–28 read as follows :

'And God said, Let us make man in our image, after our likeness : and let them have dominion over the fish of the sea, and over the fowl of the air, and over the cattle, and over all the earth, and over every creeping thing that creepeth upon the earth. So God created man in his own image, in the image of God created he him ; male and female created he them. And God blessed them, and God said unto them, Be fruitful, and multiply, and replenish the earth, and subdue it : and have dominion over the fish of the sea, and over the fowl of the air, and over every living thing that moveth upon the earth.'

These verses provide the essential clues to the way in which the relationship between man and nature developed in the western world-view, and their importance can scarcely be over-emphasized. Before we can proceed, however, to examine the various concepts and attitudes of mind to which they have given rise, two general problems of interpretation require discussion. The first concerns the use of a biblical text like this one for the purpose of illuminating the elements of a world-view, the second concerns the form in which God's instructions were conveyed to man.

The material in these chapters of Genesis sets out to provide an acceptable explanation of the existence of the world, of man, and of man's place in the scheme of things, all matters for which no *rational* (or as we might be tempted to put it today, no *scientific*) explanation was readily available. In some way, man had to come to terms with these events, and, even before the development of scientific theories of the evolution of man and the age of the earth made *literal* acceptance of the biblical account of the creation untenable, these creation stories were seen by many as some sort of parable. Similarly, advances in geology made biblical chronology obsolete, so that it was no longer possible to accept Bishop Ussher's date of 4004 B C as that of the creation of man (or to perpetuate usefully the long-standing argument about the season of the year in which the creation took place.). The 'literal' accuracy of the mythological sections of the narrative

is not an issue : it is totally irrelevant to an examination of a
world-view ; what *is* important is that the mythological explanation provided the context in which they lived. Even
could it be shown that its fantasy content was known, or at
least strongly suspected, its acceptance as the approved explanation determined the attitude which was blended into
the other components to form the Hebrew world-view in
its totality. No matter to what extent the literal explanation
of creation given in the Biblical narrative was subsequently
demolished by advances in knowledge, its function in the
formation of our world-view remains unaltered. Modern
science has, of course, substituted a different and, to us, a
more rational and acceptable model of the origins of man,
though this has been brought about only slowly and with
difficulty. On the other hand, no advances in scientific
theory have, or, indeed, could have, replaced other aspects of
Judaic mythology, notably those relating man to his environment, such as the idea of man's dominion over the rest of
nature, which is still today a central component of western
world-view. Those sections of the creation legends which
provide explanations for what must have happened should
be distinguished from those which suggest a mode of conduct, since these two facets became sharply differentiated
with the passage of time, however much they may originally
have been seen as all of a piece.

The other point to be discussed is the form in which God's
purposes for man are handed down to him. The two instructions which are of greatest relevance in an ecological context
are 'Be fruitful and multiply and replenish the earth', and
'Have dominion over the earth and subdue it'. These two
injunctions are conveyed in the mythological material as
direct commands from God to his people 'Be fruitful and
multiply!', 'Have dominion over the earth!'. It is highly

improbable, to say the least, that these statements represented the *earliest* attitudes of man to his environment, but were rather the rationalizations of a people of relatively advanced technology, certainly in the post-domestication of plants and animals stage, projected backwards to the imagined time of the creation. While these phrases can be interpreted as they stand as direct commands, they can also be seen as projections of what was to take place in the course of human history, given the benefit of hind-sight. For instance, in his commentary on Genesis, Cassuto elucidates the first phrase, 'Be fruitful and multiply', thus : 'Although you are only two, yet, through your fruitfulness and increase, your descendants will fill the land and subdue it'. No such comment specifically accompanies the other injunction 'Have dominion over the fish of the sea, etc.', though it is likely that Cassuto intended 'and subdue it' to cover the second phrase as well. Nevertheless, the intended functions of these two phrases are inseparable ; either both must be taken as commands, or both as prophecies. One cannot be interpreted in the first way, and the other in the second.

Is there, however, a real or significant distinction between these two interpretations, the injunction and the prophecy, as they have been differentiated here? I believe that there is not, and that they both come to very much the same thing. Looking backwards over a period of time, the Hebrew people recognized that a great increase in their number had occurred, and that a continual process of environmental control had accompanied it as the necessary technology had developed. With their concept of history as the working-out of the divine purpose, there could be little difference between God's 'Do this' and His 'This is what will happen' : in both ways of expression, man's licence is established and it does not really alter if it is put across as command or forecast. Since God

knew what was to happen in the future, commands and fore-
casts were essentially the same thing ; hence there is no
conflict between the two interpretations. I believe that
Cassuto is undoubtedly correct in commenting as he does.
Be this as it may, the sense of man's right to dominate nature,
and to multiply his species, took their places in our world-
view in the earliest times. Whatever changes have come
about in the rest of our attitude to the world, *dominion* and
multiplication have persisted and have indeed been intensi-
fied.

The result of this view of nature as subordinate to man's
requirements has been to set man apart from the rest of
nature, in a hierarchical system, God : Man : Nature. Man
came to see himself not as part of nature but outside it. Consequently, harmony within nature, as exists in certain other
religions, has never been a lasting ideal to which western
man aspired ; it was rather a totally irrelevant concept, and
one which probably took hold of western imagination only
rarely. The extraordinary complexity of modern environmental technology, and the increasing ability to apply it, for
good or ill, to other planets, as well as to the earth, has resulted
from the fundamental role in which western man has seen
himself, as the controller of nature. There has, of course, been
an intensification of control, resulting from the increasing
ability to intervene in natural processes, but this is a matter
of degree ; it does not require, nor has it involved, a change in
our basic attitude. Even if the dominion of man over nature
reaches a *reductio ad absurdum otiosum,* with the destruction of the habitable earth, no change in attitude will be
needed. I propose to argue that the present situation arose
because although a number of concepts which might have
controlled the way in which man used his dominion over
nature were developed, for one reason or another they fell

into desuetude. Once the limits on dominion were removed, an ecological breakdown was inevitable.

This sense of complete control is implicit in the phrase 'replenish the earth and subdue it'. The Hebrew word translated in the Authorized Version as 'subdue' is elsewhere used for the military subjugation of conquered territory, and clearly implies reliance on force. (Compare Numbers, xxxii, 20–22 : 'And Moses said unto them, If ye will do this thing, if ye will go armed before the Lord to war, And will go all of you armed over Jordan before the Lord, until he hath driven out his enemies from before him, And the land be subdued before the Lord...'). With this meaning, *subdue,* in the sense of treading down, is a very powerful expression of man's attitude to the rest of nature, and suggests that he sees himself in a position of absolute command. Such an intensity of feeling, and the implied appeal to force, possibly reflects the difficulties of surviving in a semi-arid or even desert environment rather than in, say, a tropical rain forest or the well-watered savanna country in which *Homo sapiens* probably evolved. Life in the environment in which the Hebrew tribes found themselves was hard and precarious, and remains so to this day, despite the great advantages of modern technology. Extremes of weather, both diurnal and seasonal, cause much discomfort and rain comes infrequently ; when it does come, it falls, often heavily, on parched soil which is easily eroded. Vegetation is sparse and the soil, once denuded, stays exposed for long periods. It is scarcely surprising that centuries of wrestling with such stubborn conditions found expression in a context of subjugation.

Having created man, and having instructed him to subdue the earth, God proceeds to set forth man's relation to nature in the clearest possible terms (Genesis i 29–30) :

'And God said, Behold, I have given you every herb yielding seed, which is upon the face of all the earth, and every
tree, in the which is the fruit of a tree yielding seed ; to
you it shall be for meat. And to every beast of the earth,
and to every fowl of the air, and to every thing that creepeth
upon the earth, wherein there is life, I have given every
green herb for meat : and it was so'

Remembering the old Elizabethan use of the word 'meat' to
include all food, not just animal flesh, we note that God
allocated seeds and fruits to man, and green plants (or,
rather, the green parts of plants) to animals. The addition of
animal flesh to human diet was made only later, after the
Flood. (It is perhaps worth mentioning here the comment of
Novatian, as quoted by Wallace-Hadrill, 'meat was added to
man's original diet of fruit as cultivation of the soil demanded
more robust food'!) These original dietary instructions go
further than enjoining man to restrict himself to a vegetarian
regime, and deny the existence of any carnivorous animals,
which, as is now known, certainly preceded man on earth.
Plants are to be shared between man, who eats seeds and
fruits, and animals which eat leaves and stems.

It seems that in this passage the author is attempting to
portray some type of ideal existence, a paradise in which the
taking of life for food was not necessary, so that any trophic
level above the herbivorous cannot be allowed for. It is perhaps strange that a distinction should be drawn between
plants, which could be eaten, and had, presumably, no life,
and animals, which could not be eaten and *had* life. This
remained a vision of an ideal existence, but when faced with
reality, man's dominion over nature took precedence. Respect for the *life* of plants has not been part of the western
ethic (*pace* Samuel Butler's *Erewhon*), though there is a
certain magnificence and appearance of permanency about

trees that catches the human imagination. By contrast, man's awareness of his biological relationship to the rest of the animal kingdom is apt to intervene in the process of dominating nature, as seen, for instance, in the nature teaching of St Francis, in Schweitzer's principle of 'Reverence for Life', in evolutionary humanism or as an essential component in the rise of the modern conservation movement.

The role of man in exploiting nature, and his place in the hierarchy of creation, are referred to again and again in the Old Testament, but nowhere in more expressive terms than in the 8th Psalm : 'Thou madest him to have dominion over the works of thy hands ; thou has put all things under his feet : All sheep and oxen, yea, and the beasts of the field ; The fowl of the air, and the fish of the sea, and whatsoever passeth through the paths of the seas'. For all that God had made man in his own image, a phrase to which we will have to return in the next chapter, and had given him an unique place in nature, the Old Testament is full of doubt about man's position, somewhere between the two extremes, 'a little less than God' and 'man, that is a worm'. The author of Ecclesiastes vigorously puts forward an earthy view of man :

'I said in mine heart concerning the estate of the sons of men, that God might manifest them, and that they might see that they themselves are beasts. For that which befalleth the sons of men befalleth beasts ; even one thing befalleth them : as the one dieth, so dieth the other ; yea, they have all one breath ; so that a man hath no preeminence above a beast : for all is vanity. All go unto one place ; all are of the dust, and all turn to dust again. Who knoweth the spirit of man that goeth upward, and the spirit of the beast that goeth downward to the earth?' (III 18–21).

Although the theology of this book has been described as

'strange' and 'difficult', it is one which might, if properly examined, be found to have a peculiar appeal to the so-called 'post-Christian' age of the twentieth century, both in the type of problem dealt with and the solutions put forward. I suspect that it is likely to be precisely those elements which have been the most difficult to assimilate into orthodox Christianity that would arouse the greatest contemporary interest.

Although man has seen himself as licensed to dominate the earth, he has not been able to accept completely and wholeheartedly this place in the hierarchical arrangement God : Man : Nature. The uneasiness arising out of this arrangement and man's attempt to fill a certain niche in it has been most severe in his relationship with animals, perhaps because of obvious biological affinity and the way in which increasing anatomical, physiological and psychological knowledge have tended to make this affinity greater rather than lesser. Having dominion over every living thing that moves upon the earth may be a satisfactory enough concept in theory, but in practice it has not been at all easy to establish. In particular it has been difficult to draw a line between two extremes—on the one hand, hunting and killing an animal for food, or exterminating a pest or a competitor and, on the other, making a friend of a household pet or caring for an injured animal. Strangely enough, there is striking evidence of the existence of this same conflict of attitude to animals in the first two chapters of Genesis, between the Priestly version (I 20–26) and the Jahwist version (II 7 ; 19) of the sequence of the creation. In the Priestly version, God, having separated dry land and sea, and having covered the earth with grasses, herbs and trees, then created fishes, birds, terrestrial animals and, finally, man. In the same verse as that in which man was created, he was given dominion over all those living creatures which had preceded him in the order of creation. In the other (and, significantly, earlier) version, God made the earth, but since there had been no rain, there was no vegetation on it. Following the mist which watered the earth, preparing the soil surface for plant growth, God created man, and then planted a garden for him to live in. Only then did God feel that man should not live on the earth alone and created the animals and birds as companions for him. Finding these inadequate for the purpose, since although they could be a *help* to man, they could not be *meet* for him, that is, suitable for him or equal to him, God made a woman from Adam's rib, and brought her to him. Nowhere in the Jahwist narrative of the creation is man given dominion over the animals ; the only instruction he receives is that, with one important exception, he might eat freely from every tree in the garden.

I do not wish to suggest that the juxtaposition of these two contrasting and even contradictory versions of the creation legends have been the cause of our subsequent ambivalence towards the animal world ; such a suggestion would be a grave distortion of the use of Biblical texts. Rather I see the existence of these two opposing views of the relationship between man and animals as evidence that the problem is a very old one, and that as long ago as the compilation of Genesis there was sufficient ambivalence of attitude to ensure that both versions had to be put forward. In one of these, the utility of animals to man was stressed ; in the other, a recognition that they could be companions for him, though not to the extent that another human being could be. The failure to reconcile these two strands of feeling are obviously of great antiquity, and persist to this day as a component of such problems as far apart as the preservation of animal species threatened with extinction and the development and future of 'factory' farming.

In a wider context, a marked dualism can be recognized in man's attitude to the whole of nature, control and dominance versus mystical awareness. Some of the latter may well have been associated with the fear of the unknown in societies of simple technology, and as the extent of the unknown (and, hence, uncontrollable) has shrunk, the sense of domination has grown. The changing attitude to mountain landscape, for instance, has been fully documented, and discussed with great sensitivity, by Marjorie Nicolson in her book *Mountain Gloom and Mountain Glory*. Even within the same society, different and conflicting attitudes can co-exist, and the same individual is not necessarily consistent in his state of mind. A mystical awareness of his natural environment may still be experienced by the most hardened and sophisticated sub- duer of nature in the present technological era, for instance in response to the cathedral-like atmosphere of the depths of a forest, in the solitary surroundings of a deserted moor, on the sea, or, most readily perhaps of all, when flying alone at night in a cloudless sky. In such circumstances, dominion over nature seems almost irrelevant, not to say irreverent, and the sense of the insignificance of human activity seems overwhelming.

This might suggest that an awareness of the majesty of nature depends on a situation beyond the technical compet- ence of the beholder, but this is not necessarily so, as anyone who has ploughed a field with a team of horses knows per- fectly well. However, the exploitation of nature by techno- logical means almost certainly presupposes an attitude of dominion. The development of the techniques needed to control the environment have been accompanied in western thought by an attitude of dominion, explained in mythologi- cal terms as an injunction from the Creator. The combination of licence and ability provided the justification needed for increasing control and would, if unchecked, lead inexorably to the destruction of the habitable world.

4

The Concept of Stewardship

A society which includes amongst its earliest and most tenaciously-held beliefs a concept of its right to dominion over nature is faced with a paradox : the fullest exploitation of nature involves its eventual destruction. The destruction of nature involves, too, the destruction of that society itself. Man's belief in his right of dominion over nature may be based on the role of the rest of nature as providing the resources needed for his own survival, but when this attitude is expressed in terms of a direct injunction that nature is his, to be subdued and conquered, the need for a system of contrasting beliefs which would operate to hold exploitative policies in check becomes urgent. There is thus set up a pair of opposite and contradictory positions which must in some way be reconciled if a society is to be maintained in equilibrium with its resources, and may be epitomized as a conflict between long-term and short-term interests.

It is as well to recognize the fundamental knife-edge on which the management of all biologically-based resource systems must rest. If successful management be deemed to be that level of exploitation which permits a steady flow of products over the longest possible period of time visualized by the society (possibly stated as 'in perpetuity', but usually considered unconsciously in terms of finite periods), it is possible to maintain a level of production which does not involve a deterioration in the system itself, and may even improve it. This rate of flow could, on the other hand, be greatly increased if the concept of sustained yield over long periods of time be abandoned, and a much higher rate of production achieved in the short-term. This would result in a reduction in the productivity of the resource system, perhaps even to zero if the process were to be continued long enough. A simple analogy can be made with money in the bank : either you can live off the interest, leaving the capital intact, or you can increase the flow of money from your account by removing interest and a proportion of the original capital — with obvious implications for the future of *that* particular resource system. If the exploitive process is arrested before the system is completely ruined, a period of rest may permit a return to a fully productive condition, but this must by no means be taken for granted. For most, probably all, eco-systems there is a point of 'no return' beyond which restoration is no longer possible.

The risk of over-exploitation is particularly serious in those environments frequently referred to as 'fragile' or as 'ecological tension zones', where the ecosystem is so delicately balanced that a level of human intervention that would be appropriate and harmless in more favoured circumstances quickly becomes disastrously disruptive. Western civilization was cradled and developed in just such tension zones — in the Near East, under semi-arid conditions, dependent on low and erratic rainfall, with high rates of evaporation and a sparse vegetative cover, quickly eaten out and slow to recover from even moderate exploitation ; and on the erosion-prone landscapes of the Mediterranean area, where the hot dry sum-

mer is followed by heavy rains which wash the soil from un-
protected hillsides. These fragile environments in 'problem'
climates are above all others in need of protection from un-
controlled human exploitation ; the survival of societies then
depends in large measure on the philosophical and technical
means which can be developed to ensure the necessary degree of protection.

The essential paradox remains ; dominion over nature is
incompatible with long-term sustenance. Only if the subjugation of nature is not permitted to proceed all the way to
complete domination can a system of secure management be
perpetuated. How can such subjugation be held in check,
how can the claims of moderate, long-term production be
maintained against those of higher production obtained by
'mining' the resource system itself ? The life and thought of a
society may involve a number of uneasy compromises between
what is ideal and what is possible, and its world-view has to
face up to many contradictions ; in our civilization, the conflict between short-term and long-term concepts of management is just one such contradiction. If society is to continue to
function, such contradictions have to be avoided or resolved,
and if it is not permissible to state explicitly that the ideal
is not possible (and it may be considered unwise to formulate such a view, however obvious it is), it may have to be
wrapped up in mythological terms and an acceptable reconciliation of opposing and contrary positions thus put forward. This chapter, and the next three, are devoted to study-
ing various ways in which western civilization has attempted
to solve this problem.

The Hebrews achieved this reconciliation by evolving a
concept of man's responsibility to God for the management
of the earth, a concept which was duly carried over into
Christianity, becoming part of the western heritage. If a view

can be inculcated that man is only looking after the world on behalf of some extra-terrestrial presence such as a God or Gods, the contradictions in the concept of dominion over nature can be softened by a feeling of responsibility, and a reason provided for holding exploitative tendencies in check. Responsibility for managing the world is thus a mediating factor, in the mythological sense, providing a fulcrum between two opposing positions, and was readily acceptable within the context of the rest of the world-view of Hebrew and Christian society.

Isolating 'responsibility to God' in this way as a mediating factor in the mythological sense brings us back to the function of mythology in the development of a world-view. To speak of 'responsibility to God' in this way is not intended to reduce religious arguments to the level of fairy stories : applying mythological concepts to these situations merely provides an alternative basis for judging the significance of theological concepts in guiding the developing thought of a society. The statement that the Hebrews *evolved* a concept of responsibility to God for the management of nature is in no way in conflict with the Biblical texts, but is a particular interpretation of them—perhaps a different way of looking at them, and one which may be new and superficially strange to people who have been used to taking religious systems at their face value. The argument here is crucial to the whole purpose of this book ; I am suggesting that the apparent conflict between dominion over nature and long-term environmental stability was mediated for a long time by the elaboration of a sense of responsibility to God for the way in which man was to exercise his dominion. When in the course of history a sense of responsibility to God lost its hold on society, these constraints were removed, or replaced by others, differently based ; the concept of responsibility remained.

It is now necessary to examine the evidence for this feeling of responsibility, and to trace its development within the context of the early Hebrew world-view. In the Jahwist account of the creation of the world (Genesis II 15), we read: 'And the Lord God took the man, and put him into the garden of Eden to dress it and to keep it'. We already know what the garden was like (although the author probably visualized it more as an oasis)—it contained every tree that was pleasant to the sight and good for food. This description is extremely interesting, because it acknowledges that man's demands on nature are not restricted to food and nourishment, but include also amenity. Indeed, amenity is put before sustenance. This description draws attention to a further tension between opposing positions, because, as we now know all too well, extreme control over natural ecosystems, based on the requirements of intensive food production, is usually found to be incompatible with the maintenance of high standards of amenity. Amenity is usually the first to suffer, reversing the Biblical order of pleasant to the sight and good for food.

Man's first duty was to *dress* the garden—that is, to till it, to manage it, presumably for both pleasure and profit. His second duty was to *keep* it. By 'keep' here I understand not *preserve*, in the sense of putting on one side for future use, but *protect*, preventing harm, in the same sense as the word is used in Isaiah, XXVII 3, 'I the Lord do keep it (His vineyard); I will water it every moment: lest any hurt it, I will keep it night and day'. The burden of the passage in Genesis is clear enough: God put man into the world in order that he should look after it. The ultimate ownership of the world was never for a moment in doubt, as evidenced, to take one out of many examples, by the words of the Psalmist, 'The earth is the Lord's, and the fulness thereof; the world and they that dwell therein.' (Psalm 24). Man is frequently reminded of his subordinate position ; he may have been put on earth to look after it, but there is no suggestion of ownership at the time of the creation, nor is there any suggestion that in the course of time man might come to inherit the earth for himself, for instance as a reward for good management. Accordingly, the conclusion must be that the Hebrews believed that one reason for man's presence on earth was that he should look after it *on behalf of God.*

In the Priestly version of the creation of the world there is parallel evidence, of a different type, concerning the relation between God and Man in the management of the earth. Genesis I 26 begins thus : 'And God said, Let us make man in our image, after our likeness' ; and verse 27 reads : 'So God created man in his own image, in the image of God created he him ; male and female created he them.' This is a text notoriously leading to differences in theological interpretation, and Altmann has recently discussed the wide gulf which separates Jewish and Christian opinion on the meaning of these few words. 'In the image of God' clearly implies a distinction between man and the rest of the created world, man being modelled on a divine creator, and, as Brandon remarks, it suggests a view of man possibly influenced by Mesopotamian ideas that man was created to serve the Gods, 'an idea which finds reflection, if perhaps not so overtly, in Hebrew thought'. Man was also differentiated from the rest of creation in that he alone had the ability to reason, to use his intelligence and to act upon his conclusions. I find myself also drawn to the view that 'Homo imago Dei' equally implies that man is to act in a responsible way in relation to the lower orders of creation, in the same way as God acts towards man. This, I believe, is implicit in the hierarchical system *God : man : nature.* It could be argued that the exploitation of the earth, even to its ultimate destruction, can be justified by the juxtaposition of two concepts—man as having been granted dominion over the rest of nature, and man as having purposely been given intelligence by his creator. One concept tells man what he should do, the other how he should do it. This argument would hold that having created man, God proceeded to sit back and watch him destroy the earth as part of the divine plan—a cynical view of the creation that is not in keeping with the rest of Hebraic world-view, with its trust in God, albeit a strict and at times vengeful God, and its sense of a chosen people fulfilling God's purpose for the world. It brings us close to an even more difficult argument, that the gradual destruction of the earth was itself part of the Divine purpose.

'In the image of God' is better interpreted not only as setting up man as a little lower than God, but also as sharing an identity of interests and responsibility. As God keeps *His* vineyard, so should man keep his. It is, of course, a facile basis for atheism that inverts the phrase into 'Man created God in his own image', God being thus explained away, but such an argument misses the point ; the phrase can *legitimately* be inverted to give a two-way sense of responsibility. It is what the Hebrews *believed* about the creation of the world that matters ; if they saw themselves as having been created in the image of God, they then knew something about the unknowable, and by personalizing God in this way they were able to achieve an equivalence not only of outlook but also of action. Man could thus see himself responsible and accountable to God for the proper management of the earth, over which he had in turn been given complete control. In other words, man saw himself as a steward.

It is interesting to note here that the concept of man as a steward of the earth, acting there on God's behalf, has a central place also in the Islamic faith. In the Qur'an (Sura 2.30), God says to the angels (who are initially rather hostile to the suggestion) 'I am going to place a *khalifah* on earth' before creating Adam. The proper rendering of *khalifah* into English is not easy in this context : Sale has 'substitute', but 'vice-gerent' or 'deputy' would appear to be more acceptable translations. The political implications of this phrase have been discussed by Watt and it is clear that the sense of vice-roy is intended ; he refers also to Sura 38.26, where God says to David, 'We have appointed thee a *khalifah* on the earth : judge therefore between men with truth'. It is clear that God was seen to place man on earth in order that he would rule it as His deputy. Concerning this interpretation, Cragg comments, 'This is the charter of man's responsible dignity, his call to mastery linked with the acknowledgement of account-ability. All things are under man and he is under God'. It seems to me that in this instance, the Qur'an has expressed one of the basic tenets of the western world-view more ex-plicitly than did Genesis, though the essence of responsibility is implicit in 'dominion' also. To quote Cragg again :

'Yet insofar as that *imago Dei* concept is fulfilled in this awareness of man as having creativity within nature and a dominion for God's sake, the absence of the term and the silence about its other Biblical significance need not be over drawn. Much of the intention of the phrase is already here. In effect the caliphate of the Qur'an *is* the dominion of the Bible : in practical senses the larger, bolder termi-nology of Genesis may be said to be implied. Mastery and control in due subordinate order within the Divine will are the essential quality of 'man made in the image of God'... The place left for man in the scheme of things is seen to be a vicegerency, where the feasibility of conquest and con-trol is discovered to be a delegated trust'.

This section of the argument can best be summed up by stating that, in relation to the resources of the earth, the people of western civilization inherited a picture of God as an absentee landlord, with themselves as His steward. The introduction of the term 'resources' in this context is not unreasonable. A component of the human environment is transferred from a neutral category to the 'resource' status when it is perceived to be incorporated through appropriate cultural manipulation into the life of man, and as a factor in his survival. Although the term 'resources' is, not surprisingly, absent from the early records of western civilization, the concept of certain plants and animals as being set apart for the particular use of man is clearly set out in Genesis. It is perhaps a little surprising that there is no explicit reference to man as God's steward in the management of the earth; possibly the concept was too important, too central to the way of life, too obvious to require any precise statement or reiteration.

The concept of stewardship is, however, reinterpreted frequently in the New Testament, in terms meaningful to the society of 2000 years ago. There are a number of parables in the first three Gospels which seek to illuminate, either directly or indirectly, the theme of man's responsibility to God for the way in which he uses the fruits of the earth. Furthermore, the use of the pastoral 'good shepherd' imagery, which suffuses the gospel stories in particular, also reflects the idea of responsibility and trust. The concept of stewardship in the New Testament goes far beyond the scope of the natural environment of man and covers man's individual responsibility for the fullest use of his personality and inherent abilities which, like tangible possessions such as land, are given to him by God, to whom he is at all times accountable. These parables differ from myths in that they do not attempt to mediate contradictions, but only to illustrate and illuminate an abstract concept by reference to every day experience common to — or at least immediately understandable by — all of those listening. The position of a steward in a household was of long standing, and can be found referred to in Genesis xv 2, where Abram speaks to God of his steward Eliezer. 'Steward' is the way in which the Authorized Version translates 'the son of the possession of my house', and the word certainly suits the later description of the 'eldest servant of his house, that ruled over all he had'. There are further references to the function of the steward in the stories about Joseph. In ancient Greece, and throughout the Near East, the steward was the man to whom the patriarch of the extended family group left all the day-to-day administration. He was responsible for the members of the family group as well as their possessions, and was obviously someone of considerable authority. When the Gospels talk of stewardship, they were dealing with a well-known facet of social structure, not an abstract concept, and the role of the steward was used to highlight the duties which all men had to accept within the whole Christian family.

An examination of these parables of stewardship in the Gospels shows that a number of them can be grouped together to confirm the Judeo-Christian attitude to God as that of the absentee landlord. All three Gospels include the story of the householder who planted and equipped a vineyard and, having leased it to an husbandman, departed for foreign parts (Matthew xxi; Mark xii; Luke xx). When he sent his servants to collect the grapes, the husbandman beat them or killed them; eventually he sent his son, but he too was killed. On his own return, he destroyed the wicked husbandman, replacing him with others who would hand over the grapes when due. Obviously this parable can be interpreted on a variety of levels, but the onus of responsibility on the occupier to discharge his obligations comes across clearly, and carries with it the lesson of what happens when that responsibility is evaded. A similar parable is found in Matthew xxiv and Luke xii, contrasting the behaviour of the good and the bad servants awaiting their master's return from a journey. The master discovers the good servant carrying out his duties in a faithful and proper manner, and marks him down for future promotion, but the bad one was caught ill-treating the other servants and spending his time drinking in bad company, having made up his mind that the master's return would be delayed. The parable of the talents, too, specifies the relationship between stewards and absent masters (Matthew xxv ; Luke xix). The stewards were rewarded according to the use they had made of the property with which they had been entrusted ; the two who had made one hundred per cent profit were rewarded, while the one who had merely kept his share intact was reprimanded and discharged. At the very least, the parable continues, he could have put the money out at interest.

In addition to those parables which refer specifically to an absent master, there are others which deal with the notion of stewardship. Thus the Christian gospels reinforce in powerful and easily comprehended imagery the Hebrew concept of man's responsibility to an absent and unseen, yet personal and all-powerful, God. The good and faithful servant is one who takes over responsibility for his master's property in his absence, keeping the family together and caring for them all. He is also expected to use the property entrusted to him in the most profitable way. More important, however, than these considerations is the accountability which is automatically introduced as part of this responsibility. The good steward is rewarded, the wicked (or even the non-profit-making) steward is punished. There is also the motive, particularly in the 'absentee landlord' parables, of the inevitable day of reckoning. Provided that the steward carries out his duties in a responsible manner, all will be well. The wicked steward prefers to proceed in the belief that what he is doing is hidden from his master, but in the fullness of time he is bound to be discovered. The obvious sense of responsibility urged on man as part of his stewardship is supported by a warning of the accountability imposed with it.

There is also a feeling that this accountability is liable to be called for when it is least expected, when, to quote just one example, the absent master is thought to be delaying his return. This emphasizes that stewardship is a continuing process, to be maintained whether one is watched over or not; it is not something which can be disregarded for a while, to be corrected later by a measure of additional work. The overall impression left by these parables of stewardship is that man's responsibility for the earth is continuous and that he should not need to be frequently reminded of it. It should be a natural and even subconscious matter to use our resources, both those external and internal to us, in a productive manner ; certainly we should not embark on policies leading to their decline or decay. There can be no point in denying at this juncture that the introduction of the idea of responsibility into the *God : man : nature* relationship unavoidably implies a concept of eschatology, for the essence of responsibility is accountability. The Judeo-Christian literature is permeated with references to the day of reckoning, when man will be called upon to account for his stewardship, and though anticipation of reward or fear of retribution would not today necessarily be considered the happiest way in which to achieve a sense of responsibility for what we may do with our environment, it may perhaps have seemed to be a possible one in days gone by.

The idea that man was responsible to God for the use of the earth remained—and remains—a central part of Judeo-Christian thought, so much so that the need to formulate it in precise terms seems to have been infrequently felt. The clearest statement known to me comes from the unlikely pen of Sir Matthew Hale, the distinguished seventeenth century Chief Justice of England. In the introduction to *The Primitive Origination of Mankind,* published in 1677, he informed his readers that it had been written in odd moments over a long part of a busy professional career, in order to show that the essential truths of religion did not need to depend on revelation, but could be derived from a consideration of natural phenomena alone. Towards the end of his long book occurs the following passage :

'In relation therefore to this inferior World of Brutes and Vegetables, the End of Man's Creation was, that he should be the VICE-ROY of the great God of Heaven and Earth in this inferior World ; his Steward, *Villicus,* Bayliff, or Farmer of this goodly Farm of the lower World, and reserved to himself the supreme Dominion, and the Tribute of Fidelity, Obedience, and Gratitude, as the greatest Recognition or Rent for the same, making his Usufructuary of this inferior World to husband and order it, and enjoy the Fruits thereof with sobriety, moderation, and thankfulness.

'And hereby Man was invested with power, authority, right, dominion, trust, and care, to correct and abridge the excesses and cruelties of the fiercer Animals, to give protection and defence to the mansuete and useful, to preserve the *Species* of divers Vegetables, to improve them and others, to correct the redundance of unprofitable Vegetables, to preserve the face of the Earth in beauty, usefulness, and fruitfulness. And surely, as it was not below the Wisdom and Goodness of God to create the very Vegetable Nature, and render the Earth more beautiful and useful by it, so neither was it unbecoming the same Wisdom to ordain and constitute such a subordinate Superintendent over it, that might take an immediate care of it. 'And certainly if we observe the special and peculiar accommodation and adaptation of Man, to the regiment and ordering of this lower World, we shall have reason, even without Revelation, to conclude that this was one End of the Creation of Man, namely, to be the Vice-gerent of Almighty God, in the subordinate Regiment especially of the Animal and Vegetable Provinces.'

In Hale's view there was clearly no escape from man's responsibility to God for the proper management of the earth, to control the wilder animals and to protect the weaker, to preserve and improve useful plants and to eliminate weeds and, be it noted, to maintain the beauty as well as the productivity of the earth. Was it entirely a coincidence that, like the author of Genesis, he put beauty before utility? Man's ability to carry out these duties appeared to him as evidence for the purpose of his creation, and, given Hale's legal training, it is not surprising that he viewed the situation within the contractual framework with which he was in everyday contact, 'steward, villicus, bailiff, or farmer'. The elements of contract—rights and obligations, responsibility and accountability—are inherent in the Judeo-Christian attitude to man's role on earth, even if there is little explicit statement of this general theme. There is, however, a parallel system in a man's individual responsibility for his personal property, and the obligations imposed thereby, an examination of which throws additional light on the wider problems of stewardship.

5

Responsibility for Property

The concept of stewardship as a mediating factor between man's use and his abuse of nature through the subsequent history of western civilization is an abstraction which probably had less hold on the individual than the practical stewardship required of him for the proper use of his own personal property. From the latter it is possible to argue by analogy that, as man should care for his own resources, so should Man care for his.

It may be argued against this view that the management of private property is so hedged about by legal and similar considerations that any analogy that could be drawn between man and Man in this regard would be false. This is not so ; legal institutions such as property may appear stable and immutable over the centuries, and the institutions themselves may indeed be so, while their social functions may become completely transformed. Changing social conditions lead to changes in the interpretation of institutions, and not vice versa, so that for purposes of practice, the law follows changes in the outlook of societies. Technical innovations which arise, for instance, as a result of the application of science to natural processes do so within a given legal and institutional framework, and will be mirrored eventually in appropriate changes in that framework. Technical progress is achieved *within* a given legal system, and not as a result of that system, and may well lead to development of the *apparatus* of the system without changing its essence.

It is true that a considerable delay may occur before this transformation comes about, and it is right, as well as probably inevitable, that such delays should occur. If they did not, the law would have to carry a load of vacillation more burdensome than its reflection of past conventions. Although the law may pretend to stand aloof from the requirements of society, this is a pose, though one which is readily understandable. It may, indeed, be a useful pose, in that it isolates legal institutions from too rapid oscillations in response to social changes. The dependence of legal institutions on social considerations was elegantly put by a great American lawyer, O. W. Holmes, as follows :

'The very considerations which judges most rarely mention, and always with an apology, are the secret roots from which the law draws all the juices of life—I mean, of course, considerations of what is expedient for the community concerned. Every important principle which is developed by litigation is in fact and at bottom the result of more or less definitely understood views of public policy ; most generally, to be sure, under our practice and traditions, the unconscious result of instinctive preferences and inarticulate convictions, but none the less traceable to views of public policy in the last analysis... it will be found that when ancient rules maintain themselves..., new reasons more fitted to the time have been found for them, and that they gradually receive a new content, and at last a new form, from the grounds to which they have been transplanted.'

If it may be accepted that changes in the social function of property reflect changes in the world-view of societies, it is appropriate to examine those changes in the individual's responsibility for his own property as a guide to the more general proposition of how society as a whole sees itself to be responsible for the management of *its* natural resources. Returning to the main currents of western thought, Judeo-Christian teaching on property can be summarized in two statements : first, property is necessary for the fullest development of the individual, although the extent to which one can acquire private property may need to be restricted by considerations of public interest ; second, the individual is responsible to God as trustee for his property.

In the early days of the settlement of Palestine by the Hebrew tribes, property, consisting of persons, land and possessions, was owned not by an individual but by the family, and was the responsibility of the head of the family, the patriarch. The meaning of *the family* is important, as it covered the family as a concept in time, so that the administration of its property had to take into consideration the effects of management on future generations. It would seem on first sight an inflexible system, not permitting the dispersal of property even under economic distress, but it was recognized that in practice property might have to change hands. Where there was no relative to claim the property for the family, an opportunity was provided every seven years for the discharge of debts, and a special occasion in the Jubilee year, which occurred every 50th year, on which land and other property could be returned to the original family. Whether or not the Jubilee year was strictly observed seems to be debatable, but the intention was clear. The sanctity of property is so firmly established in the Ten Commandments that a recognition of the social problems resulting from a departure from these rules must be assumed.

The balanced patriarchal system gradually broke down as the strong traditional family and other social groupings eroded under the impetus of the increasing prosperity and urbanization which accompanied the rise of the monarchy. The time of David marked the highest point of the traditional culture, when it was still possible for the king to exult, 'for all that is in the heaven and in the earth is thine ; thine is the kingdom, O Lord, and thou art exalted as head above all. Both riches and honour come of thee, and thou reignest over all ; and in thine hand is power and might ; and in thy hand it is to make great, and to give strength unto all' (I Chronicles, XXIX 11–12). However well-poised such a system may seem in theory, in practice it required strong and self-denying leadership if the greed and ambition of individuals were not to lead to social disruption. The history of post-Davidian Israel illustrates this ; despite the strict laws against alienation of property, subsequent kings began to see the land as their own, to dispose of as they wished. Remember Naboth's reply to the king who coveted his vineyard : 'The Lord forbid it me, that I should give the inheritance of my fathers unto thee' (I Kings, XXI 3). Whereupon the King proceeded to obtain it by treachery (encouraged by his wife, who was a princess of Tyre, where a much more authoritarian regime held sway). The social picture began to change from a fair distribution of land and resources to one in which large areas were concentrated in the hands of a few people, leading to the all-too-familiar pattern of a few wealthy landowners and many landless dependants.

This is a situation which typically results in social unrest and protest, and it is interesting to see what some of the more vocal critics of that era had to say about it.

'Woe unto them that join house to house, that lay field to

field, till there be no place, that they may be placed alone in
the midst of the earth! In mine ears said the Lord of hosts,
Of a truth many houses shall be desolate, even great and
fair, without inhabitant' (Isaiah v 8–9).

'Forasmuch therefore as your treading is upon the poor,
and ye take from him burdens of wheat : ye have built
houses of hewn stone, but ye shall not dwell in them ; ye
have planted pleasant vineyards, but ye shall not drink
wine of them. For I know your manifold transgressions
and your mighty sins : they afflict the just, they take a
bribe, and they turn aside the poor in the gate from their
right' (Amos v 11–12).

'Woe to them that devise iniquity, and work evil upon
their beds! when the morning is light, they practise it, because it is in the power of their hand. And they covet
fields, and take them by violence ; and houses, and take
them away : so they oppress a man and his house, even a
man and his heritage' (Micah, ii 1–2).

The roots of this conflict are to be found in the tensions inherent in the twofold role of property, which is a means of
personal identification as well as a trust accountable to God.
This double role implies that a balance needs to be struck,
individual enjoyment against social requirements. The need
to establish this balance between private and public property
rights, and the extent to which the balance swings between
the two extreme positions, recur again and again in the
history of resource management. Many of the problems
facing the western world today are those of readjustment
following a shifting of the balance, this time towards the
position of increased emphasis on social requirements.

The teaching of the New Testament on the responsibilities
inherent in the ownership of property has already been dis-

cussed, but the early Church Fathers were clearly very worried about the actions of man in appropriating the earth and its products for individual use. They argued that since individual greed was one of the consequences of the Fall of Man, the establishment of private rights of enjoyment of property was the only way in which an individual's requirements could be safeguarded. In their view, the resources of the world were originally intended to be available to all mankind in a system of commonality, a position of balance between private and public property rights leaning heavily towards the public extreme, but a system which was liable to favour the strong at the expense of the weak. St Ambrose, who lived in the second half of the century AD, said :

'Our Lord God intended the world to be the common possession of all men, and that it should produce its fruits for all, but covetousness has portioned out individual rights of property. It is just, therefore, that if you claim something for yourself as a private person which was bestowed upon the human race, every living soul of it in common, you should at all events distribute some of it to the poor, so that you do not deny food to those to whom you owe a share of your legal rights.'

This is an interesting argument, as it introduces the problem of the extent to which a man is entitled to appropriate the fruits of the earth beyond his own personal requirements, and St Ambrose insists on the individual's responsibility to his less fortunate fellow men. The later development of this idea was to lead to the furtherance of alms-giving as a system of poor-relief, and the rationalization of charity as justifying the accumulation of wealth.

Gregory the Great, 200 years after St Ambrose, put the matter more succinctly : 'Our property is ours to distribute, but not ours to keep ; we have no right of waste, and no right to withhold from those who are in need'. The first and the last sections of this statement made the same points as did St Ambrose, but the second, that we have no right of waste, is something new and different. It suggests a concept of sound management which has a modern ring, one which has never yet been properly accepted. 'Waste' goes further than the obvious connotation that we should avoid letting surplus products decay, but includes the idea that we should manage our property in the most efficient way, so that the yield from the 'capital' is maximized.

While St Augustine, in the fourth century, had argued that without the protection offered by some socio-political organization, property as a working institution could not persist, the fullest development of a concept of property which combined Aristotelian political justification and Judeo-Christian theology is to be found in the works of St Thomas Aquinas, in the thirteenth century. St Thomas set down the framework of a definition which sought to establish the containment of private property rights by social obligations. His views are so important for an understanding of what was to be man's attitude to nature in subsequent centuries that extensive quotation is justified. The following three extracts come from Quaestio 66 of the *Summa Theologica*, in Dawson's translation. First, in relation to man's control over nature :

'Material things may be considered under two aspects. First, as to their nature : and this in no way lies within human power, but only within the divine power whose wish all things obey. Secondly, as to the use of such things. And in this respect, man has a natural control over material things ; for he can, in virtue of his reason and will, make use of material things for his own benefit, as though they were created for this purpose : for imperfect things exist to serve the advantage of the more perfect as we have already seen. On this principle the Philosopher proves (I, Politics), that the possession of material things is natural to man. And this natural dominion which man has over other creatures, in virtue of reason which makes him the image of God, is clearly shown in the creation of man (Genesis I) where it is said : "Let us make man to our own image and likeness, and he shall rule over the fish of the sea," etc.'

Second, on private rights of property :

'With respect to material things there are two points which man must consider. First, concerning the power of acquisition and disposal : and in this respect private possession is permissible. It is also necessary to human life for three reasons. First, because every one is more concerned with the obtaining of what concerns himself alone than with the common affairs of all or of many others : for each one, avoiding extra labour, leaves the common task to the next man ; as we see when there are too many officials. Secondly, because human affairs are dealt with in a more orderly manner when each has his own business to go about : there would be complete confusion if every one tried to do everything. Thirdly, because this leads to a more peaceful condition of man ; provided each is content with his own. So we see that it is among those who possess something jointly and in common that disputes most frequently arise.

'The other point which concerns man with regard to material things is their use. As to this, men should not hold material things as their own but to the common benefit : each readily sharing them with others in their necessity.'

And, thirdly, on the duty of charity :

'What pertains to human law can in no way detract from what pertains to natural law or to divine law. Now according to the natural order, instituted by divine providence, material goods are provided for the satisfaction of human needs. Therefore the division and appropriation of property, which proceeds from human law, must not hinder the satisfaction of man's necessity from such goods. Equally, whatever a man has in superabundance is owed, of natural right, to the poor for their sustenance.'

Reading these passages in the context of his other writings on similar matters, St Thomas' position is explicit: natural law provides that material things are provided by God for the use of all men ; human law requires that a system of private property be set up for the management of material things ; the use of property must be limited to that which is reasonable for the individual. He recognized that man's highest development was to be achieved in a political organization that could regulate and direct human endeavour. Elsewhere he stated that 'man is naturally a social and political animal, destined more than all other animals to live in a community', and his teachings pointed the way to a design for living in a state of economic organization of which the basis was Christian ethics.

The theological and philosophical definition of the legitimate extent of property rights, which reached its clearest expression in St Thomas Aquinas, was supplemented by the way in which European society was organized in the Middle Ages. Under the conceptions of the older Roman world-view, the possession of property had not involved the assumption of social responsibility, but this attitude did not survive the development of feudalism. It was replaced by the feeling that the enjoyment of wealth and privilege carried with it the responsibility for public affairs. Laymen frequently think of feudalism as being an arrangement for rapid and effective mobilization in times of war, and this may well have been one of the primary considerations, but it went much further than this ; responsibility for local government and the administration of justice were important functions of the feudal lords. (Do we not find a reflection of this attitude in Rousseau's *Confessions,* where he says that as a young man 'A single castle was the limit of my ambition. To be the favourite of its lord and lady, the lover of their daughter, the friend of their son, *and protector of their neighbours*' [my italics]?) Medieval agricultural economy, in which much of the land was held a in form of corporate ownership, survived for many centuries because the lord of the manor, through his steward, maintained a close supervision of the villagers and the way in which they worked the land. Without such supervision, the maintenance of fertility would have been impossible, since in any system of commonality it does not pay the individual to hold back in the interests of future production if his actions are going to be vitiated by those of his competitors. Nevertheless, these were centuries of rapidly expanding technology, particularly in the use of new or improved sources of energy, and this resulted in the transformation of established patterns of land use and an increase in the rate of urbanization. This has been thoroughly and wittily discussed by Lynn White in his fascinating book, *Medieval Technology and Social Change,* in which he draws attention also to the way in which the increasing sense of the domination of nature is reflected in the calendars.

'The old Roman calendars had occasionally shown genre scenes of human activity, but the dominant tradition (which continued in Byzantium) was to depict the months as passive personifications bearing symbols of attributes. The new Carolingian calendars, which set the pattern for the Middle Ages, are very different : they show a coercive attitude towards natural resources. They are definitely

Northern in origin ; for the olive, which loomed so large in
the Roman cycles, has now vanished. The pictures change
to scenes of ploughing, harvesting, wood-chopping, people
knocking down acorns for the pigs, pig-slaughtering. Man
and nature are now two things, and man is master.'

The transition from the mental atmosphere of the Middle
Ages to that of the modern world took several centuries, and
incorporated far-reaching changes in resource use, population and economic organization. The extent of the technical
control of the environment which Europe had achieved at the
end of this period of transition depended on parallel developments in social and political institutions, and could not have
occurred under the strict application of the principles laid
down by St Thomas Aquinas. His ideal of a society whose
conduct was to be guided by Christian maxims, with their
limitations on the ownership of property and their condem-
nation of usury, was incompatible with the nature of the
economic development looked for. This is really the crux of
the matter : Christian rules of social conduct stood in the way
of economic development. Either the rules had to be relaxed
or economic development had to languish. Had the rules
been sufficiently flexible, and had those people in authority
been prepared to work within them, they might have been
gradually adapted to meet the changing problems of the
times, but this did not happen. Instead, as we can see now,
there came about a shrinkage in the areas of human conduct
covered by the existing principles, with economic and commercial activities being gradually removed from the domain
of traditional ethics. The key to the situation is probably to
be found in the erosion of the authority of the teachings of
the church and the waning of faith which were part of the
secularization of the western world-view, too large a subject

to be discussed here. As the sphere of influence of the Church over the many different aspects of human life shrank, restrictions in the extent and manner of the accumulation of wealth and property imposed by Christian ethics were removed.

Because this change in the authority of the church took place at the same time as the rise of Protestantism, a relationship between Calvinism, in particular, and capitalism was suggested by Max Weber, and has been widely debated ; the conditions for the development of a capitalist system were further discussed by Tawney in his book *Religion and the Rise of Capitalism,* to which anyone interested in this subject is particularly referred. Weber's theory was that Calvinism developed a personality well suited to the accumulation of riches, but efforts to establish a causal relationship tend to overlook the fact that a capitalist, acquisitive spirit was nothing new. For instance, the rise of modern business methods, such as the introduction of the double-entry bookkeeping system, had occurred much earlier, in Catholic fourteenth-century Europe. People had acted in a 'capitalist' manner for centuries, but in doing so were not acting in conformity with strict Catholic social ethics, and there must have been considerable tension between materialistic and religious claims on individual conduct. In any case, in Gellner's words, 'historians now cite Scots Highlanders or Hungarian aristocrats who were Calvinist without becoming capitalist or Italian merchants who were capitalist without becoming Calvinist'. The dilemma of the would-be capitalist is neatly established in a quotation Tawney makes from Benvenuto da Ismola, whom he describes as a medieval cynic : 'Qui facit usuram vadit ad infernum ; qui non facit vadit ad inopiam' (He who takes usury goes to hell ; he who does not, goes to the workhouse).

Eventually the position was reached when religious constraints were considered not to apply to everyday affairs and,
in particular, to the making of money, and the stage was set
for the development of the institutional framework without
which it would not have been possible to translate into
practical terms man's growing conviction that his task on
earth was the furtherance of his dominion over nature. In
this way, the first restriction on the accumulation and unfettered manipulation of property, that of Christian ethical
discipline, was removed, but the change in attitude which
resulted was essentially negative : the right to unlimited
property was permitted because the earlier rules were held
not to apply. Positive justification for the appropriation of
property was an important accompaniment to the mercantile
society of the seventeenth century ; we can usefully study
the argument put forward by Locke, as it was to have great
influence on the development of western thought and institutions.

Justification of the establishment of private property-
rights themselves was neither new nor difficult, and had been
made perfectly adequately by St Thomas Aquinas, as we
have seen. Locke's particular contribution was to provide a
justification for *unequal and unlimited* individual appropriation, which is a very different matter. The first edition of
the *Two Treatises on Government* appeared anonymously
with the date 1690, that is, 13 years after Hale's *Primitive
Origination of Mankind,* although the two books betray
completely different attitudes of mind ; Hale's seeming to
belong to a remote era, Locke's looking forward to our own.
Individual ownership as the most efficient means of land
management was taken for granted, but Locke was faced with
the need to justify the accumulation of land surplus to the
requirements of the owner himself. To do this he had to over-

come two objections ; the first, that a man should not possess
so much property that in his use of it some wastage of the
products might result, he removed by introducing into the
argument the concept of money, money not being itself
subject to spoiling. The second objection was that the con-
centration of ownership in a few individual hands would
reduce the resources available to the rest of the population,
and this Locke set aside by claiming that large-scale management increased overall production. He founded his theory of
property on the argument that a man's labour is his own, to
do with as he liked (recalling Hobbes' *Leviathan*, 'A man's
labour also, is a commodity exchangeable for benefit as well
as any other thing'). The importance of this view that a man's
labour is his own property lies in the relation of the individual to the society of which he is a member. If a man's labour
is his own, to do with as he pleases, society is not involved : if
the right to unlimited property rests on personal labour,
property rights no longer carry social obligations. Thus
another set of restrictions on the unfettered accumulation of
property, that demanding that property rights carried with
them social obligations, was also set aside, and the way was
clear for the worst excesses of the industrial revolution.

The emancipation of property rights from religious or
social constraints has not, of course, gone unchallenged over
the last three centuries. For instance, the limitation of self-
sufficiency recurred in writings of the nineteenth century
utilitarians ; J. S. Mill, though satisfied with the concept of
private property, held that with land, ownership should be
conditioned by expediency ; access and enjoyment should be
limited to that which is necessary for efficient exploitation.
The Christian view has always been that man is but a steward
of the property with which God has entrusted him, and this
view has been restated in recent times by Pope Pius xi in the

Divina Redemptoris thus : 'Considering themselves only as stewards of their earthly goods, let them be mindful of the account they must render of them to their Lord and Master'. Or, in a Protestant context, in the Report of the Proceedings of the Oxford Conference of 1937 : 'All human property rights are relative and contingent only, in virtue of the dependence of man upon God, as the giver of all wealth and as the creator of man's capacity to develop the resources of nature'. The last phrase is of especial significance, as it links property rights and the world's resources, emphasizing that the development of these resources is itself the gift of God and, hence, part of the stewardship of man.

6

The Role of the State

It seems a far cry today from the belief that the resources of
the world are held by man on trust, and that he is accountable
to God for the use he makes of them ; we have become so
accustomed to the all-pervading influence of central government over so many aspects of everyday life that we may find
it difficult to realize the extent to which our contemporary
mythology has allowed the state to usurp many of the functions previously allocated to the Deity. Hence we have now
reached the position when the individual is expected to look
on his property as on trust to him from society, to whom he is
responsible for the way he manages it. But it was not always
thus : 'The great and chief end therefore', wrote Locke, 'of
mens uniting into commonwealths, and putting themselves
under government, is the preservation of their property. To
which in the state of nature there are many things wanting'.
The ideal state of man was the 'state of nature', in which there
would be no restrictions on individual behavior or freedom
of action, but since in the everyday world this was not a
workable proposition, a modicum of organized government
was a necessary evil, in order that the rightful enjoyment of
private property might be preserved. Locke proceeded to

argue, further, that since the only justification for the existence of the state was the preservation of private property, the state could not then turn round and separate an individual from his property (and by property in this context he included 'lives, liberties and estates').

Under such a concept of government, the sanctity of property rights was so assured that not even a popular majority decision could upset it, since the preservation of property was itself the *raison d'être* of the state. Furthermore, property rights were seen to have primacy over human, social or economic requirements, an attitude which formed the basis of much international legal thinking and of the principles of economic development. This primacy of property rights has increasingly been challenged, even in countries like the United States or Great Britain, where it has had greatest influence, as well as having been rejected by countries which have been exploited under political and economic systems arising out of it. Accordingly it has led to tension where different notions of property and economic development have come into conflict. A good example of this conflict is to be found in the attempts of Mexico to gain some measure of control over its oil revenues, which, in the 1930s, were almost entirely under British or American control. These attempts ran head-on into legal and philosophical concepts, whatever Woodrow Wilson might have had to say previously about human rights being above property rights. Northrop comments on the situation in the following terms :

'Under these circumstances even the most elementary attempt upon the part of the Mexican Government to establish economic justice within its own country by regaining some of its natural resources would appear to the United States and Great Britain, as it did to Woodrow Wilson in 1916, as a breach not merely of traditional international

law but also of the elementary principles of political
morality'.

An even more striking instance of the same attitude was to be
seen in the outraged reaction of Britain and France to the
Egyptian take-over of the Suez Canal in 1956, and the extent
to which public opinion (in these and other countries) had
moved away from the Lockean position can be gauged from
the measure of support they received for their opposition.
These tensions may be brought to the surface also, as we shall
see, in domestic as well as in international circumstances,
since, as social philosophy has evolved, traditional ideas
about property have stubbornly resisted assimilation.

We can now see that there has been a major development,
which has proceeded at an ever-increasing tempo, from the
Lockean principle of unfettered rights over property towards
a situation of social responsibility, as the role of the state has
moved more and more towards intervention in the economic
and social life of the citizen. Today, the western world has
reached a position almost diametrically opposed to Locke's,
but the radical change in outlook goes much further than
rights in physical property alone. While in previous centuries
there was a gradual shrinkage in the area of responsibility of
the church, so that matters of economic and commercial
significance were increasingly excluded, we can now trace a
contrary motion in which the state, starting with a concern
for just these matters, has gradually widened its coverage to
include aspects of personal welfare as well. In this way we
have come to accept the position of the state as the ultimate
authority to which the individual owes a duty for the management of the natural resources 'entrusted' to his care. This
change in attitude has, naturally enough, proceeded at different rates in the various countries of western civilization,
and has gone much further in some countries (for instance,

the Netherlands or Great Britain) than in others (such as the
United States), depending on the traditional attitude to
centralized government and, ultimately, on their population:
resource balance. However unpopular the view may be, we
should recognize that the new approach to the ownership of
resources and the responsibility attendant upon it, which has
been referred to as 'fiduciary ownership', is not so far removed from the traditional Christian attitude as might
appear at first sight, despite the complete secularization of
responsibility, the state having been substituted for God.

This change was a natural accompaniment to the increasing intervention of the state in the internal management
of its resources. I do not propose to enquire here into the
origins and influence of the concept of the state, but from the
viewpoint of the trends in social responsibility, a turning-
point was reached in the philosophy of writers such as Saint
Simon, Comte and those influenced by them, with the demands for the total planning of all economic aspects of the
organization of the state if the progress of man was to be
assured. Their views were particularly important within the
context of that section of western thought which equated
progress with the increasing material well-being of individual
men and women. Once it became accepted that the centralized direction of socio-economic development was a proper
area of state administration, the Lockean approach to the
unrestricted enjoyment of private property was doomed,
since the cardinal principle of the state existing to safeguard
and preserve such enjoyment was broached. As far as the
underlying changes in attitudes to the responsibility for the
management of a country's resources is concerned, it does
not really matter whether the new trend developed within a
democratic society by peaceful social evolution towards an
increasingly 'socialized' condition, or by the violent intro-

duction of a Marxist-type organization. Under the latter system, of course, the ownership of resources is explicitly vested in the state, in order to prevent them falling into private hands, in which they could be exploited for personal gain, against the interests of the community as a whole.

There are two important ways in which the intervention of the state through its economic planning has influenced the management of resources in western society. The first of these has been a direct and legislated interference by the state into the freedom of the individual to plan the use which he makes of his property. Although I am particularly concerned here with the use of land and with the regulation of land- and water-based industries, and the effect of physical planning and co-ordinated regional development in preempting land usage, amenity considerations written into modern town planning regulations are in every way comparable. With the present densities of population, it is inevitable that executive action must be available to provide the land required where roads and other installations have to be built, airports constructed or housing provided. The general adoption of the principle of zoning land for specified purposes ties an owner's hands very greatly, and certainly affects the market value of his property. Although compensation is usually provided where land is taken over, this does not alter the fact that the owner and his property are being separated, possibly under duress. Even if the compensation is fair and the appeal procedure adequate (neither of which assumptions would necessarily be held to be valid), the fact remains that the Englishman's home is no longer his castle, and it would no longer be possible to uphold Blackstone's dictum—'Regard of the law for private property is so great... that it will not authorise the least violation of it, not even for the general good of the whole community'.

Apart from the direct and obvious ways of state intervention in land use, there are many other restrictions placed on a land owner, designed not only for direct economic purposes but on behalf of conservation interests, the maintenance of scenic beauty or the protection of wildlife. Such restrictions range from the type of trap or poison permissible for the control of vermin to the movement of land between parallel uses, such as between agriculture and forestry. Many of these regulations are of course both necessary and welcome, and are aimed at preventing the further deterioration of the environment, an outstanding example being the limitations on the use of the persistent chlorinated hydrocarbon insecticides ; whether these regulatory powers are right or wrong, they set sharp limits to the authority of the manager and could only have arisen in western society when the Lockean tradition had been replaced with one giving government the right to control the use of property.

The second important social change is the amount of land now held directly by Government departments, public agencies and the like. In Great Britain, Government Departments such as Agriculture, Housing and Local Government, and Defence ; quasi-Governmental bodies such as the Natural Environment Research Council (particularly via the Nature Conservancy), the Forestry Commission, the National Coal Board ; hydro-electricity undertakings ; local government organizations ; and such bodies as the National Trust probably together own more than four million acres of rural land, though the degree of dependence on, or independence from, state control obviously varies. When the land owned by large commercial concerns such as insurance companies or manufacturers is added to this total, it is easy to see that an increasing proportion of the resources of the country has moved from personal to corporate ownership. (It may be relevant here to recall the massive land-holdings of the Church at the time when its influence over personal conduct was at its height.) This process of land consolidation under state aegis has gone much further in Holland than in this country, and it has been estimated that the Dutch government owns or controls directly about 25 per cent of all the land resources. The various countries of the western world are all moving in the same direction, with increasing proportions of the land coming under government control, though in some of them the trend still seems to be bitterly contested.

The movement towards central authority is to be found not only in the ownership of land, or in the power of the state to direct the form of usage which is to be followed, but also in the elaboration of a concept of social benefits as a determinant of the assessment of land use. The forestry industry provides a very good example of this. The primary purpose of forest management would, at first sight, seem to be obvious enough—the production of wood for constructional or pulping products. This was not always the role of forests—in earlier days they existed mainly as royal hunting grounds— but over the last century or so, when the efficient management of a forest resource was developed on a firmer scientific and economic basis, a single-purpose timber-oriented attitude has become dominant. However, a closer examination of the contemporary role of forests in the national economy reveals a number of benefits other than timber : the protection of threatened areas from erosion; the safeguarding of water catchment grounds ; the preservation of wild life ; the aesthetic improvement of landscape ; and, of particular and growing importance, the provision of recreational facilities. These purposes have come to be known as 'social benefits', and involve the forestry industry in a number of problems peculiarly difficult to solve. The demands of some of these social benefits may be irreconcilable with the maximum production of wood; for instance, they may bring many more people into the forest, with increased risk of fire, and involve the provision of picnic sites and a degree of supervision of visitors; for aesthetic reasons, species may have to be planted which would not otherwise have been chosen; it may be necessary to tolerate a degree of wildlife damage, as for instance by deer browsing, which reduces the annual increment of wood and may prevent the establishment or regrowth of young trees. The real trouble goes deeper: it is not that a system of management has to be evolved to accommodate these various demands, but that the benefits accruing from them cannot be directly costed and expressed in economic terms in the same way as can the production of timber.

Thus in requiring the forest manager—whether in the public or the private sector—to accept the responsibility of providing social benefits, the state is, on a superficial analysis, reducing the profitability of the resource system, since it involves an apparent reduction in the economic return on the capital invested. This is clearly illusory, and obviously results from a deficiency in the technique of economic assessment applied to forestry enterprizes; were it possible to calculate the value of these social benefits in pounds, shillings and pence they could be accounted for in the measurement of the return and the profitability of the whole enterprize might well in certain circumstances be shown to increase considerably under a suitable multipurpose objective. As yet there are no direct methods generally applicable for the economic assessment of social benefits, though there are some indirect ways in which estimates may be made, but it is probable that a residue of 'imponderables' will always remain, however sophisticated the calculations may become. The position of those responsible for the efficient management of forestry enterprizes is obviously difficult, and their bargaining position vis-à-vis other industries for a share in the capital market severely restricted, if they are required to provide unmeasured social benefits in addition to directly marketable and easily valued products. This restriction is particularly hard on the private forestry investor, who is likely to resist a move towards the acceptance of 'social benefit' management—one result of which is to encourage demands for the extension of state enterprise over 'recalcitrant' elements of the private sector.

It could be argued that the fault lies in the evolution of a view of social responsibility which sees the management of natural resources as proceeding for the benefit of the state, with social benefits taking precedence over the economic interests of the owner. I believe that this is not so ; the concept of 'fiduciary' management has come about slowly and is obviously a workable way of allocating responsibility for the use of the world, compatible with the rest of the contemporary world-view, although it is anathema to some sections of the community. The fault lies elsewhere, in that we have not yet elaborated a satisfactory economic 'accounting' system to equate direct and indirect benefits. We might well require a system which could not be achieved by tinkering with existing procedures but which might involve sweeping away many basic attitudes to capital investment and return. Since investment in land and other environmental resources is only one part of a much larger complex of financial priorities and allocations, it is not at all easy to see how this might eventuate without a wholesale reorganization of the economic framework of society. A possible compromise would be the formulation of agreed, if arbitrary and partially untestable, valuations of the indirect benefits which could then be applied to the various enterprises involved.

A particularly revealing illustration of the development of the social responsibility incumbent on the management of natural resources in Great Britain arose out of the Agriculture Act of 1947. In return for a system of agreed prices and subsidies, the efficiency of the agricultural industry was to be assured by the strict regulation of those farmers and estate owners whose management persistently fell below the acceptable standards of good husbandry, as judged by their colleagues in their own districts. Provision was made for advice, supervision and even direction, but in the last resort the farmer could be dispossessed of his holding, though not, of course, without appropriate compensation or right of appeal. In the ten years in which the Act was in force, 4,200 farmers were put under supervision and 377 dispossessed, while a smaller number of estate owners was similarly penalized. The clear implication was that agricultural resources were considered to be too valuable to the state for them to be allowed to remain sub-optimally productive. As a reward for guaranteed economic stability this measure of control was in fact accepted, even welcomed, by the farming community as being quite reasonable, though there can be no doubt that certain cases involved great personal hardship.

These provisions in the Agriculture Act of 1947 were probably some way ahead of their time, and in the event they foundered, in part at least, on just the rock we might expect, the principle of the supremacy of property rights. (There were other rocks, including a widespread dislike of delegated legislation and certain aspects of procedure.) The Courts were obviously reluctant to uphold the provisions for dispossession under the Act, in some instances giving the impression that they were prepared to look for technicalities with which they could come to the aid of the farmer threatened with the loss of his home and his livelihood. In one case, where George Benney had been served with a dispossession order, Lord Justice Denning said :

'The farm is his sole means of livelihood and he has no other place to live. Yet a dispossession order has been made against him, turning him out of the land of which he is the owner and out of the house where he has lived all his life, with no provision made for alternative accommodation or other work. His only offence, if it is an offence, is that he has not maintained a reasonable standard of production on the holding... He was bound to leave his home and his land unless he could find some technicality on which to upset the proceedings.'

Having drawn attention to such a technicality, he continued 'but technical though it is, I think that Benney is entitled to take advantage of it'. The workings of this act provide a most interesting commentary on the responsibility incumbent on resource management in contemporary western society, and have been thoroughly explored by Self and Storing in Chapter 5 of *The State and the Farmer,* from which the quotation of Lord Justice Denning has been taken. There is no doubt in my mind that given the present trends in the relationship between the state and its resources, similar provisions will be enacted at some time in the future when public opinion (and, for that matter, judicial opinion) will have moved more firmly towards the acceptance of the implications of social responsibility.

One of the areas in which man's attitude to the world is changing most quickly is the growing demand for the use of land to provide facilities for outdoor recreation. The development of recreation in the British countryside since the war has been quite unprecedented, and may be attributed to increased leisure, more money and improved means of transport (forgetting temporarily that the motor car threatens to ruin the very countryside which it opens up), as well as the changed social climate, in which access to the country by underprivileged city-dwellers is seen as a necessary measure of social justice and public health. Almost invariably, the development of recreation facilities clashes with traditional forms of land management, and a reconciliation may not be easy to find. Sometimes the conflict is between recreation and existing use on land owned by the State, for instance in proposals to develop ski-ing on a Nature Reserve, when attempts to control traditional access can arouse intense public opposition, but privately owned land is more frequently involved. Even walking over hill country, surely one of the most simple forms of exercise and enjoyment, can be severely damaging to sporting interests at particularly vulnerable times in the year. Ownership as such may not always be directly involved, as in the use of inland waters, where water-ski-ing, sailing, fishing, swimming and water management are not mutually compatible. There are many practical problems still to be worked out, but the implications of recent British legislation such as the Countryside Acts is that access to the countryside is not to be restricted by private ownership, that land has a social value which can take precedence over the economic purpose for which it is being primarily used. Land is the heritage of the people, and considerations of private enjoyment, of no matter how long standing, are not to be allowed to stand in the way.

Obviously a balance has to be struck, somewhere between enjoyment and use, at which access ceases to be harmful. It is one thing to permit, even encourage, recreational access to a tract of relatively underused hill country, quite another to allow people to picnic in the middle of a field of wheat or barley in ear. Once the principle of access has been established *as of right,* as it now seems to have been for 'unproductive' land, the point at which it is held becomes capable of discussion and variation, so that at some time in the future we can envisage access as being extended, let us say, to grassland and thence to arable land, depending on the interplay of social and economic pressures. It is even more important to realize that since access to relatively unproductive land has become socially acceptable to the point of embodiment in legislation, farmers and managers of other intensive landbased productive systems owe their immunity not to a right derived from ownership or possession, but to the voluntary and, perhaps, capricious sanction of society.

The present position is not so much that individual managers of resource units see themselves as being responsible to society, or to the state, for the way in which they look after a 'sacred trust'; this is, however, the position expected of them by everybody else, and the great majority of the people come under this category of 'everybody else'. Bearing in mind the history of the way in which responsibility for the use of resources has been allocated in western civilization, and the need for some mythological awareness of the restrictions to be placed on individual action, it seems to me that increasing pressure of population and higher standards of living can only intensify this trend towards the control of the state over its natural resources. This control can take two forms, either the overt take-over by the state, through purchase or even appropriation, of the country's resources, or the insidious, covert assumption of direction based on a doctrine of social responsibility. This trend towards administration based on 'duty to society' is not, be it noted, confined to the management of land and similar resources, but is spread widely over all spheres of human activity. An outstanding example of this is seen in the gradual if erratic development of the 'welfare state', with its greatly increased social involvement and investment of state finance in the care of human beings, in such matters as housing, medical care, employment, or attention to the elderly or other groups of 'socially deprived' persons, a movement of responsibility, again, from the private to the public sector. There is an underlying assumption that the responsibility for the welfare of the individual can no longer be left to himself, or to his more fortunate fellows, but that the onus of looking after him, from the cradle to the grave, rests upon society as a whole. Such transfers of responsibility are not new ; at one time responsibility rested heavily on the parish, leading to many abuses and militating severely against mobility of labour (it is interesting to note the recurrence of the same problem in contemporary 'Common Market' Europe, in which the increased mobility of labour has drawn attention to the different levels of social benefits in the various countries). Considerations of public health and social justice led to massive reforms, from the second quarter of the last century onwards, when the central responsibility of the state was translated into administrative machinery to form the origins of the welfare state. Sturdy beggars are no longer returned to their parish, though they may be refused entry to states other than their own.

In addition to the notion of social responsibility for the management of land-based resources and for people, there is parallel evidence for the growth of the role of the state in the provisions for industrial development and reorganization, where again the underlying assumption that the country's secondary production enterprises are too valuable to the economy to be allowed to go unsupervized, or to remain at the whim of the individual entrepreneur. The nationalization of important industrial processes is even more striking evidence of the same trend. All the evidence, from widely different contexts, points to the same conclusion—that we are expected to owe a duty to the state for the way in which we operate. While this doctrine may increase *national* efficiency, it may well turn out to be contrary to *international* organization, but perhaps in the fullness of time a unified world may take the place of the state in human consciousness, just as the parish gave way to the state.

If this notion of social responsibility continues to grow, a number of problems will grow with it. Inevitably it will involve the development of more (and, it is to be hoped, improved) administrative machinery if operational efficiency is to reach and be maintained at a high level. On the one hand there is the question of who is to make the necessary decisions. 'Society' as such has no individual voice, and cannot make decisions of itself ; it has to be represented in such a way that powers of decision-making are delegated to one man. He in turn has to delegate his powers, or appropriate portions of them, to his subordinates, and by the time they reach the individual manager they may well not represent the views of the majority of society. Hence the progressive alienation of the manager from the whole process of decision-making, even where his own 'property' is involved. Added to this are the personal difficulties of his position in a period of acute readjustment—the new concepts of social responsibility are likely to run directly counter to traditional education, background and, frequently, personal inclination. The position of 'trustee to society' is not easy to define, even once it has been accepted as a working principle, and 'society' may often appear indifferent or even hostile to his efforts, so that the manager comes to feel himself isolated within the community of which he is a member. This is particularly serious for the manager of land-based resources in an industrial country where the majority of the people has no understanding of or interest in what he does, and in which the centre of social gravity lies in the large conurbations.

On the other hand, reference to the state as the guardian of resource use, notably against over-exploitation, may turn out on analysis to be less effective than might initially be thought. Duty to society is a nebulous concept, interpretable only in terms of the decisions of that society ; there is no external frame of reference to which the actions of society can be held accountable. There is, to be sure, an *internal* system of reference, by which the organization of society can be adjusted, but there can be no restraint on resource exploitation if society itself favours, or is prepared to countenance, policies which can only end in deterioration. These policies may be the result of ignorance or short-sightedness, but often arise from a determination to sidestep informed opinion in the interest of temporary expediency. 'Jam tomorrow' is rarely as attractive a proposition as 'Jam today'. As Niebuhr has often emphasized, the replacement of private ownership by state ownership, such as is a central doctrine of Marx-Leninism, in no way provides a plausible alternative to the Christian concept of responsibility : 'Bourgeois property theory', he writes, 'has no safeguard against the power of individual property ; and Marxist theory has no protection against the excessive power of those who manipulate a socialized economic process, or who combine the control of both the economic and the political process'.

The naive belief that 'society knows best', on which these doctrines are based, is not always borne out in practice. It begs many questions, particularly concerning the processes of decision-making. Once decisions have been reached, how are they to be put into effect? How can a policy of sensible resource management, which involves present sacrifice, be put across to the majority, who are both spatially and intellectually removed from the resources on which their survival depends? These are major problems of politics and social psychology, but on their solution depends the future of the human race.

7

Population and Resources

At some stage of their evolution, human societies have to pass from a situation in which population is maintained in equilibrium with the available resources by a variety of feedback mechanisms, similar to those operative in naturally-occurring animal populations, into one in which this restriction no longer holds. Wynne-Edwards, in his exhaustive treatment of the social behaviour of animals in relation to resources, writes : 'The elaborate and highly perfected self-regulating machinery, which man used to possess like other species, has all gone by default, so utterly indeed that its former existence may seem new rather difficult to credit : though the evidence of controls everywhere exercised by primitive tribes ... will be found to admit of no other conclusion.' Although the evidence of population control in preliterate people is readily available—Devereux devotes a whole book to the use of abortion alone, citing over 400 communities—its existence is not always recognized ; perhaps the only instance widely known today is the way in which elderly or sick esquimos commit suicide in order to reduce the society's claims on a limited food supply. To take just one example, Firth's study of the people of Tikopia in the Solomon Islands revealed a population of about 1250 on 3 square miles of land surface—a high ratio, necessitating the use of marine as well as terrestrial resources—and a tendency for this population to increase. In addition to some abortion, there were four checks used to restrict continuing population growth : contraception by *coitus interruptus ;* infanticide, each couple having one boy and one or two girls, with subsequent children killed ; celibacy of the younger males (the method popular in Ireland after the great famine) ; finally, massacre—there is one instance known in their history of a group of people being slaughtered, and one of a group being expelled from the island (a method of dispersal and invasion of much wider significance). We are apt, too, to underestimate the technology of early societies ; surgical instruments, used for procuring abortion have recently been noted from Ancient Peru and are well known for Romano-British culture. These are remarkably sophisticated by comparison to some of the methods recorded by Devereux for primitive people, most of which seem to be variants on jumping on a pregnant woman's belly, though a wide range of treatments had been evolved, from the use of skin irritants and heat applied externally to drugs of plant and animal origin taken internally.

The maintenance of a balanced population : resource ratio by such mechanisms for regulating populations appears to be lost as society develops, and technical sophistication permits increased control of the resources available. Attention is thus diverted from stability to change, and the world-view alters accordingly. Emphasis is thereafter placed on the ways in which an increasing population can be catered for, and the increase itself is taken for granted or, eventually, actively encouraged. The practices which had hitherto contributed to stability are forgotten and even condemned.

We are apt to forget the extraordinary length of time which elapsed between the development of the different types of subsistence economy which have characterized the evolution of human society. Each step forward has involved a change in the technical control of the environment, something for which archaeological evidence is often available, and, presumably, a change in population, for which it is usually not. According to recent economic argument, relying on studies of existing 'primitive' resource management systems in Africa and Asia, technical change does not usually come about until forced on a society by increasing population pressure. So little is known of the factors which operated to limit the management of natural resources that an analysis of overall population densities over large areas from the limited available data of the number of persons dwelling together in particular sites is extremely dangerous. At the low population densities of the earliest subsistence economies, and the low rates of interest associated with them, the growth of populations must have been very slow.

A useful survey of the early development of agriculture is to be found in Piggott's *Ancient Europe* (Chapter 2), on which I have based the summary which forms the rest of this paragraph. Europe seems to have been colonized from the Near East about 30 or 40 thousand years ago by a people ('modern man, as handsome and wise as us', claims Piggott) who used simple flint tools and weapons. Their way of life, a migratory hunting system based on reindeer, seems to have changed little until the retreat of the glaciers, about 8,500 years ago, suggesting that the population remained in equilibrium with its resources over a very long period, perhaps 25,000 years, during which a gradual build-up of numbers occurred, and the resources became increasingly fully utilized. Turning to the Near East, there is evidence by about 9000 B C of people in Palestine, living in caves or houses, with a hunting economy using the gazelle. They do not seem to have relied on any domesticated stock, but had flint implements for cutting a crop, probably a wild or a domesticated cereal. By 7000 B C, goats had been domesticated and a cereal crop cultivated. A similar pattern of land use extended into South-East Europe, and at a date before 6000 B C there is evidence from Thessaly of a people growing wheat, and barley, flax and probably millet, with sheep (predominantly), pigs, cattle, and dogs. By 5000 B C we find evidence of peasant communities throughout this area living in permanent settlements, which indicate a fairly advanced agricultural economy, and persisting for some 3,000 years.

There would seem to be something of a paradox here ; the maintenance of a stable population : resource equilibrium by Wynne-Edwards 'self-regulating machinery' is hardly compatible with the view that an increase in population acts as the necessary spur to the introduction of improved technical control of the available resources. It may be argued that, as population pressures increase, the feed-back control of numbers should have swung into operation, keeping the population in balance with resources ; instead, attention was concentrated on technical development. We are faced with an apparently insoluble conundrum of the 'which came first, the chicken or the egg' variety ; does increased population result from improved technology, or *vice versa ?* The answer probably lies in the long time span over which these pressures build up, so that both sides of the population : resource ratio develop side by side. As population increases, attention turns to technological development, and even marginal improvements permit further increases in population, however small, while the continuing enhancement of the more specifically human characteristics of man, such as the sense of the value of life, lead gradually to a world-view in which unconsidered adjustment of population by social behaviour is left far behind.

It is interesting to find that an awareness of the pressure of population on resources is deeply imbedded in the world-view of primitive peoples. Schwarzbaum, in his essay 'The overcrowded earth', surveyed a wide range of cultures and drew attention to the widely held view in such peoples that some way has to be found to prevent population from outstripping available food supplies. In many creation legends, the death of an individual human being was initially considered to be an abnormal event, often rationalized as the necessity forced on mankind by the risk of overcrowding. He concentrates on those elements from a vast collection of myths and folk-tales which connect the arrival of Death in the world with a Malthusian-type situation of over-population and its consequent risk of starvation. Typically, populations rise until famine occurs, when the appropriate God or Gods are petitioned for some relief. This often takes the shape of the withdrawal of immortality by the imposition of disease or other inflictions, and may involve a conflict of some sort between Gods supporting life and those preferring to establish death. Similarly, there are numerous tales in European and other folklore of death being tricked into a container such as a bottle or a barrel, until the resultant increase in population overburdens the earth and famine ensues. It then becomes necessary to release death from bondage for the sake of the continuing future of the human race. The apparently widespread reliance on the Malthusian situation as forcing a limit on personal immortality is understandable, since such societies live, generally, near the limits of subsistence, and are aware from everyday experience how erratic and unreliable are their sources of food.

Bearing this in mind, it is at first sight surprising to find such a different attitude in the Hebrew world-view, where a continual expansion of population is looked upon as right and proper, even ordained. ('Be fruitful and multiply and replenish the earth', says the Priestly version.) The explanation of this contrast seems to lie in the changes in outlook which had occurred by the time at which the accounts of the creation were written down, by which time the Hebrews were clearly no longer 'preliterate', because there is evidence of a more traditional attempt to account for death in the Jahwist version of the creation, details of which may be found in a number of studies of the 'Fall'—S. G. F. Brandon's *Creation Legends of the Ancient Near East* provides an interesting if rather extreme interpretation. The story of the Flood may also be relevant in this context, since in the Mesopotamian version it was sent by the Gods to eliminate the rapidly increasing human species ; the Jahwist compiler prefers to describe it as a selective cull to remove evil-doers.

This awareness of the Malthusian situation seems to be in marked conflict with the later, Priestly, version of a divine injunction towards population growth, although this injunction, like the others discussed earlier, is best interpreted as a rationalization. The message of population increase comes across equally strongly : 'And I will make thy seed as the dust of the earth : so that if a man can number the dust of the earth, then shall thy seed also be numbered.' (The Lord to Abram, Genesis XIII 16). Later in Genesis, in sections written by other hands, similar beautiful metaphors are employed : 'Look now toward heaven, and tell the stars, if thou be able to number them : and he said unto him, So shall thy seed be'. (XV 5) 'I will multiply thy seed as the stars of the heaven, and as the sand which is upon the sea shore'. (XXII

17) The Malthusian echo in the Jahwist passages is clearly a remnant of a discarded world-view, incompletely assimilated in later redactions.

There is thus established early in the history of western civilization a belief in the continuing expectation of population increase, despite the evidence of even earlier fears that the population might get out of hand. There are also suggestions of the continuance of other methods of population control, since as late as the time of Isaiah we read of the Hebrews 'slaying the children under the clefts of the rocks', an indication of children being used for human sacrifices. Infanticide and human sacrifice often go together, and were certainly practised in surrounding countries at the same period of time. It also appears that infanticide by exposure was known to the Hebrews, if not actually practised by them, as the story of Ezekiel (XVI 5) tells us. These traces of population control do not conflict with the overall impression of population growth, which is, indeed, unusual in nomadic desert tribes which are constantly faced with the burden imposed by additional children in an economy almost continuously stretched almost to breaking point, and commonly rely on abortion. However, the Hebrews did not belong to a stable population : resource system, since they were invaders in a new land, and numbers were obviously crucial to survival.

It is only from the time of Christ that reasonable estimates of world population can be arrived at ; by that time it had reached about 250 million, having increased gradually over a long period. A useful summary can be found in Clark's *Population Growth and Land Use*. From then on there is increasing evidence of a developing attitude to, and understanding of, the rise in world population. The spread of Christianity, with its emphasis on the sanctity of human life as well as its acceptance of continued population growth, probably did little to change the situation. It is true that European countries began to drop some of the restrictive practices to which they were accustomed. Despite the efforts of Augustus to encourage population increases, abortion and infanticide were practised in Rome, particularly among the wealthy classes wishing to defend their privileges, but were treated as murder by Christians ; Philo condemned infanticide in the 1st century AD, and both Athenagoras and Chrysotom regarded abortion as murder. Wallace-Hadrill quotes St Basil as considering any distinction between a formed and an unformed foetus as inadmissible among Christians. He also said that abortion ranked as suicide, since any such attempt is usually fatal to the mother, and that women who administer drugs to procure abortions were murderesses. Certainly, Valentinian made infanticide a capital offence in AD 374, but it remained common in France until Charlemagne did the same ; in Spain, abortion and infanticide were both made punishable by death in the seventh century. Though this change in attitude may have reflected Christian principles, juvenile mortality was such that the lives that were saved from infanticide were unlikely to have contributed much to the increase in world population. It may be significant that this changing attitude to human life occurred at a time when the population of Europe was in a 'trough'—the data are far from conclusive, but Clark summarized the population data for Europe as : AD 14, 39.5 million ; AD 350, 27.6 million ; AD 600, 19.3 million ; AD 800, 29.2 million ; and AD 1000, 39.1 million. These fluctuations in population could in themselves have produced the social conditions conducive to a change in attitude.

The early Christian writers did not have much to say on demography, being more concerned with other-worldly

matters rather than with the socio-economic problems of
their own age. In the early centuries of Christianity there was
a movement in favour of celibacy as superior to the married
state, but medieval writers seemed to look on increasing
numbers as a sign of God's favour, having seen in the Bible
evidence of large families. While they were prepared to defend the right of the priesthood to live in celibacy, they
implied, in Spengler's words, that 'religious celibacy did not
interfere with population growth ; for the sanctioning of
celibacy did not remove the general obligation incumbent
upon men to multiply, inasmuch as this obligation was
collective rather than individual in character, and was naturally fulfilled by the great noncelibate majority of the population.' It was only with the increase in urbanism and the
beginnings of the mercantile economy that the positive
advantages of population growth were put forward. Widespread adoption of celibacy was objected to, on the grounds
that it would restrict population growth, but the author of
the fourteenth century 'Somnium Viridarii' raised a very
interesting and percipient argument in its favour. Strangeland quotes him thus : 'Posset et esse tanta multitudo, quod
si ulterius exerceret, terra non esset sufficiens ministrare
cibum hominibus, propter quod illo tempore naturae vis et
ordo permitteret imo juberet continere.' (There could also
exist so many people that if there were to be a further
increase, the earth would not be able to supply food for
mankind, and therefore the force and order of nature would
then permit, or rather enjoin, celibacy).

Despite this recognition that a balance between population
and resources could not be taken for granted for all time, the
attitude of the next few centuries seems, in general, to have
been that populations should be encouraged to increase.
Indeed, the whole basis for an outlook on population

changed ; no longer was a large population held up as a mark of God's favour, but rather as a mark of the greatness of the state. Arguments from economics replaced those from religion. A large population was regarded as necessary for the enhanced status of the temporal powers, for the provision of an army, for the obvious benefit to the exchequer and even for the personal glorification of the sovereign. Population was important in the accumulation of wealth, and legislation was increasingly introduced to stimulate its growth. At the individual level, children were seen as a positive economic advantage, in that they returned income to the family from an early age.

This change in attitude to population needs to be seen in perspective. Firstly, on biological grounds alone, there has always been a tendency for populations to increase, as there always will be, although an increase may be held back or even nullified by environmental conditions—starvation, disease or intraspecific competition such as warfare. Increases have to be accounted for in satisfactory terms, and the change from arguments based on religion to those on economics betrays the widespread secularization of the western worldview. Religion and economics were really two different ways of regarding the same phenomenon, each satisfactory to the spirit of the age which gave rise to them.

The concern that population growth might ultimately endanger the population : resource ratio, hinted at as long ago as the fifteenth century, is usually associated with Malthus, a writer more often referred to than read today. Malthus, as Boulding has pointed out, was an economist of the front rank, but he knew little about demography and his 'Essay on Population' of 1798 did not, indeed, contribute much to that science ; it is more concerned with history and philosophy. He found it difficult to accept Godwin's and

Condorcet's optimistic views of the future perfectibility of mankind, and drew attention to the equilibrium which must act between population and resources, and the factors operating to hold this equilibrium at a particular point. If population grew faster than food production, a point would be reached at which starvation would intervene to keep the two sides of the equation in balance. An increase in food supply merely postpones the inevitable—sooner or later, population growth would be checked and 'all these checks may be fairly resolved into misery and vice'.

There seemed to Malthus to be no escape from this situation. It is often said that the Malthusian argument has been disproved by events, in that the extraordinary advances in food production have kept ahead of population, so that no preventive check by starvation has come about. This reasoning is false; the Malthusian situation has been postponed, not eliminated. There must be some limit to population under any given intensity of resource management, and the only two ways of avoiding the Malthusian postulate are firstly to rely on continuing technological advance, with the risk of breakdown in ecological homeostasis referred to in Chapter 1, and secondly to substitute for control by starvation some other limiting factor, such as rational family planning, although the social implications of this are as yet far from clear.

Malthus devoted part of his essay to the criticism of Condorcet's famous *Sketch for a Historical Picture of the Progress of the Human Mind,* a work written in the shadow of the guillotine and first published in 1795. This is a work of extraordinary optimism, which traces the development of human society from barbarism to enlightenment, concluding with a consideration of the future. In the final section Condorcet recognized that as a result of progress :

'A very small amount of ground will be able to produce a

great quantity of supplies of greater utility or higher quality... So not only will the same amount of ground support more people, but everyone will have less work to do, will produce more, and satisfy his wants more fully'. [He continued] : 'and so, as a consequence of the physical constitution of the human race, the number of people will increase. Might there not then come a moment when these necessary laws begin to work in a contrary direction ; when, the number of people in the world finally exceeding the means of subsistence, there will in consequence ensue a continual diminution of happiness and population, a true retrogression, or at best an oscillation between good and bad? In societies that have reached this stage will not this oscillation be a perennial source of more or less periodic disaster?' [And, later] : 'But even if we agree that the limit will one day arrive, nothing follows from it that is in the least alarming as far as either the happiness of the human race or its indefinite perfectibility is concerned ; if we consider that, before all this comes to pass, the progress of reason will have kept pace with that of the sciences... we can assume that by then men will know that, if they have a duty towards those who are not yet born, that duty is not to give them existence but to give them happiness ; their aim should be to promote the general welfare of the human race or of the society in which they live or of the family to which they belong, rather than foolishly to encumber the world with useless and wretched beings. It is, then, possible that there should be a limit to the amount of food that can be produced, and, consequently, to the size of the population of the world, without this involving that untimely destruction of some of those creatures who have been given life, which is so contrary to nature and to social prosperity.'

Malthus' objections to Condorcet's 10th stage—at least in so
far as the quoted passage is concerned—are twofold. First,
Condorcet saw these checks on population as delayed until a
remote future, while Malthus thought that they were almost
upon the world at the time he wrote. Second, Malthus objected to the 'unnatural' ways in which Condorcet envisaged
the necessary family planning to come about. In some ways
—such as the potentialities of improved technology—Condorcet was more nearly correct than Malthus, though we may
wonder if the progress of reason has indeed kept pace with
that of the sciences. Condorcet showed himself to be a per-
ceptive prophet of the future ; his warning of the dangers of
oscillation and his emphasis on the importance of limiting
births to avoid population control by starvation have a very
modern ring.

There are, of course, two sides to the population : resource
equation. A community living in a defined and limited area
can increase in population to a level set by the techniques at
its disposal. Increases beyond that point can come about in
two ways ; either techniques can change, so that existing
resources can be more fully used or new resources developed,
or the area from which the resources are drawn can itself be
expanded. A decision to increase the resource base does not
necessarily involve expansion of territory by conquest,
though this has happened all too often in the course of
history, but may be brought about by the development of
barter or trading. The exchange of surplus products—especially perishable products—is nothing new, going back
to the complicated rules for the division of animal carcasses
in the earliest hunting societies, and develops along recognized trade-routes as suitable means of transport opens up
the frontiers of the individual's world. The use of trading as
a substitute for the physical enlargement of a society's

resource base requires the existence of a surplus—not necessarily in food—and the appropriate level of institutional sophistication, and as reliance on trading for the support of the home population increases, so too does specialization of home production and the socio-economic organization on which the system depends.

It would thus seem that a network of reciprocal trading arrangements would gradually be constructed to link areas having complementary requirements and surpluses, but it is at first sight unlikely that such a system could provide for so large an expansion in population as has occurred in Europe since the Middle Ages, even taking into account the phenomenal rise in agricultural technology. This increase was in fact made possible by the opening up of hitherto unexploited land in other parts of the world. The breakdown of the old medieval world-picture was accompanied by the dramatic discoveries of new worlds to conquer, and the prospects of empty land, cheap labour and opportunities for personal advancement beyond those available at home tempted men to break with their old loyalties and to take up the challenge of a new life beyond the sea. It was the surplus products of these areas, specifically grown for export, which, combined with improved transport and food storage, made possible the support of populations in the old world beyond the capabilities of its own resources. The results of this policy are only now coming home to roost, in that as populations in the previously remote areas increase, the margin of surplus available for export is gradually eroding.

The attitude of societies charged with opening up new territories provides an interesting commentary on the relationship between man and resources. As the story of the development of America shows, it is only when the shoe begins to pinch that man begins to take care of what he had previously squandered. The early settlers took dominion over nature as one of the main spring-boards for action ; here was a European society transplanted, creation legends, world-view and all, to a land which was to them empty, unexploited and ripe for development. 'To the early American' wrote Redfield, 'nature was God's provision for man's exploitation'. Just as the Creator had organized the earth and everything on it, completing this task in just six days, so it was their responsibility to apply themselves to the task of organizing their own new land. It was consequently the concept of God as engineer (or, as they would probably have put it, as *Supreme Craftsman*) that caught their imagination, and the management and transformation of their environment became for them a positive matter of fulfilling the will of God. Discussing Boorstin's book on Jefferson and his circle, Redfield summed up their attitude in the following way : 'for them man's part seems to have been to carry out, by changing nature and building institutions, the divine plan so providentially set out by God to be the American's happy destiny in the new continent'. It is easy to see how to the Americans, progress through the subjugation of the earth became the overriding task of society, and why America developed a world-view more extreme than the European in enabling it to arrogate to man the creative powers formerly attributed to his maker. The explosion of technology in Europe took place in a land already well peopled and with a tradition of restraint upon exploitation which provided some safeguard for the future, however inadequate it might prove to be. In America, the land was empty and no restraints needed to be imposed. It was easier, and cheaper, to farm a piece of land into the ground, then move westwards and repeat the process, than to manage the first land properly. 'Raubwirtschaft' could be practised with impunity, and it was not till the middle of the nineteenth century that a need for the conservation of vanishing resources began to be felt.

The continuing concept of an increase in population, and the various ways in which this can be justified, is closely related, as the quotation from Condorcet's *Sketch* showed, to the belief in the progress of the human race towards a better world. Both rely on a linear rather than a cyclic idea of history, and assume the reality to us of a future stretching out progressively far beyond our own lifetime, in which the world will be peopled by generation upon generation of our own descendants. We may not believe in the eventual ending of the world, nor in a 'Last Judgment', but we do believe in the *future* of the world, and most of us would want to ensure that it is accompanied by a future for man.

Of course, a great deal depends on what is meant by progress. To most people today, thinking fairly uncritically about the matter, progress means increased happiness, or higher standards of living, or just a better or easier life, however vaguely understood. Pressed for a better answer, they might reply, an advance of civilization. There would be general agreement with the views of Comte which I quoted at the beginning of Chapter 3, 'civilization consists, strictly speaking, on the one hand, in the development of the human mind, on the other, in the result of this, namely, the increasing power of Man over Nature'. There would probably be even more general agreement with a twentieth-century geographer who defined progress, for the particular purposes of his enquiry, as 'increasing ability to dominate the forces of nature', though, to be fair to Huntington, he went on to comment that 'This may not be the highest type of progress, nor the one that is now taking place most actively'. Certainly, to many scientists and technologists, progress is still almost synonymous with increased technical sophistication, so much so that this seems to have become an end in itself rather than merely a means to an end.

It is important to distinguish between two different aspects of the idea of progress. The first of these is that there has occurred something which we can recognize as progress, that the condition of human life on the earth has changed, and has changed for the better. The second is that this change is in some way inevitable, that it will assuredly continue in the future, and that there is a steady, though perhaps irregular or uneven, movement towards perfectibility, however defined, as part of a grand master plan for the world. Under this second meaning, progress clearly involves movement towards some goal, whether this is well articulated or not, and the advance of progress can be measured by the extent to which this goal is approached. To Bury, whose book *The Idea of Progress* went a long way to establishing this second understanding of progress as a specifically *modern* phenomenon, the idea of progress meant 'that civilization has moved, is moving, and will move in a desirable direction'. It was only when other contrasting views of history had been eliminated that the idea of progress could take hold as a philosophy of history, and, although the elements of the idea could be traced back a long way, belief in it was essentially rooted in the eighteenth century. It was, for instance, incompatible with cyclic views of time, with the Greek emphasis on the unchanging orderliness of the world, or with the other-worldliness of early Christianity. When the end of the world was daily expected, any consideration of progress was irrelevant.

It is true that the word 'progress' was used as long ago as Lucretius' *De Rerum Natura* to illustrate the changes in the human situation, but Lucretius does not necessarily imply by progress that these changes are inevitably an improvement. He could draw attention to the change in man's life from a state of cringing dependence upon nature, preyed upon by savage beasts and at the mercy of the elements, alongside a vision of a mythological golden age from which there could be only a deterioration. Indeed, a reading of Lucretius' poem suggests that he saw no incompatibility here ; he exults in the condition of the happy savage and implies that what we might be tempted to call civilization was, in fact, decay. What we see as progress was to him a decline, and took its place on the great circle of the world's growth and decay.

Only when the Golden Age of man could be taken from its place in the remote past and placed equally firmly in the remote future can we begin to talk of a belief in progress. This change in outlook, looking forwards rather than backwards, is one of the most powerful impressions left by a study of the emergence of the modern world-view—for instance, Bacon's *New Organon* :

'Again, men have been kept back as by a kind of enchantment from progress in the sciences by reverence for antiquity... For the old age of the world is to be accounted the true antiquity ; and this is the attribute of our own times, not of that earlier age of the world in which the ancients lived, and which, though in respect of us it was the elder, yet in respect of the world it was the younger.' (Aphorism 84)

An attitude such as this, particularly when coupled to a conviction that the proper use of science is to improve the lot of mankind, presupposes a belief in the possibility of continuing improvement quite foreign to earlier thought.

Efforts to demonstrate the modernity of the belief in progress suffered a major and, it would seem, successful counter-attack when they were challenged from a number of points of view (a good example is Baillie's *The Belief in*

Progress, which I have earlier quoted). The basis of the idea of progress, it is now suggested, lies in the Judeo-Christian attitude to time and history, with the world moving towards a divinely-ordained and transcendent end. Baillie goes so far as to label the belief in progress 'a Christian heresy' and writes :

> 'There is almost as little doubt that the various alternative *a priori* pre-suppositions with which in the modern mind this conception has been supplied in replacement of the original Christian presupposition of the providential guidance of history towards the salvation of the race... now find themselves helpless to resist the acids of contemporary scepticism'.

At first sight it would appear to be unimportant whether the belief in progress is based on a secular view of movement towards the perfectibility of man or on the fundamental beliefs of Judeo-Christianity, since both approaches share the onward-looking movement towards the future, both acknowledge that there *is* a future for the human race which is better than the present, and much better than the past. The importance of the origin of the view lies in the extent to which it provides satisfactory motivation for our present conduct, since, if our actions are ill-considered, what we do now may profoundly affect the future of the world.

8

The Concern for Posterity

It is an interesting commentary on our use of the world that the strongly-held view that the rest of nature exists—indeed, has been specifically provided—for the sole benefit of man, to be developed by all available methods for his advantage, has been offset by some mediating concept of responsibility for the way in which the powers over nature are to be used. There seems to have been a continual striving to find some way in which a balance could be held between use and abuse, between stability and over-exploitation, expressed through the changing mythology of society, by which the opposing and often contradictory concepts can be juggled into temporarily acceptable positions. In western civilization, the belief in the right to control nature remained dominant, even intensifying as new techniques became available and as the pressure of population on resources increased, while a lasting and consistent method of imbuing a sense of responsibility for how we use this control has been less easy to achieve. It is basically a question of determining our attitude to the future of the world and the people who are to inhabit it ; the failure of western world-view to develop a really satisfactory answer to the question 'Why should we concern

ourselves for the future productivity of the world's resources?' in the face of an increasing population is possibly
the most important reason why we have now to envisage the
prospect of a deterioration in the natural environment
beyond the power of our socio-technological organization to
arrest, let alone to correct.

Nevertheless, it seems quite clear to me that we *do* concern
ourselves for the future of the world. As far as I can ascertain,
western man always has done. It may seem irrational, for we
are calling upon ourselves to make sacrifices not so much on
our own account, that we may benefit from them ourselves,
but for the benefit of generations as yet unborn. It is not
difficult for us to accept that as individuals we are well ad-
vised to take sufficient care of the world for its resources to
last out our own life-span, and also that we should project this
feeling of forethought to cover the lives of our own children,
possibly even extending it to our grandchildren. We know
our children and grandchildren as human beings, each with
an individual personality, hopes and aspirations, each, we
may feel, having a right to expect at least as much from life
and if possible more than we ourselves experience. It is when
we look even further forward into the future that we find
ourselves thinking not in terms of known and identifiable
individuals, in whom we have a personal stake, but in an
abstract, unidentifiable posterity. Some, if not the most, part
of this posterity will be the descendants of persons or peoples
whom we may heartily detest, but, for all that, we do not wish
to think of them inheriting a derelict earth. Why should we
concern ourselves about what sort of world this posterity will
inherit? Even though it may at first sight seem irrational, the
fact remains that we *do* see ourselves responsible to posterity
for the way in which we manage the earth.

The concern for posterity, as a way of mediating the use

and abuse of nature, is a concept which I have not hitherto
referred to, since it requires a prior examination of all those
other ideas which form the basis of western world-view and
about which this book is concerned—dominion, stewardship and progress. To begin with, the very notion of posterity
only achieves significance in a world-view in which a linear
view of time is predominant; only when it is possible to look
forward in full confidence to a world stretching out ahead
into the far future, a world which will be populated by the
descendants of the people now alive, can we usefully think in
terms of the rights and expectations of posterity. Where
cyclic concepts of time hold sway there can be no real concern for the material needs of future generations, just as a
society holding the material world to be evil would hardly
be expected to spare much thought or effort to its conservation. The notion of concern for posterity is thus very closely
allied to the notion of progress; both involve the same view
of the reality and significance of the future of the world, and
although the idea of progress implies a continuing and inevitable improvement in the human condition, however this
may be evaluated, a concern for posterity, at the very least, is
based on a desire to avoid a deterioration. Furthermore, just
as the idea of progress has been exposed as a sheep in wolf's
clothing, in that it is essentially a Judeo-Christian doctrine in
a secular guise, the idea of a concern for posterity may also
be damned as a Christian heresy, for both reflect—or even
replace—the central, religious elements of western civilization. These elements may or may not be consciously accepted as a part of our world-view, but they are nevertheless
tenaciously held and are capable of assimilation, as are all
such ideas, in a variety of transformations. The relationship
between progress and posterity is thoroughly and elegantly
examined by Becker in a chapter on 'The Uses of Posterity',

in *The Heavenly City of the Eighteenth-Century Philo-sophers*, which should be consulted by anyone who wishes to follow this subject further.

The 'philosophes' of the Enlightenment had, indeed, raised the notion of 'posterity' almost to the status of a religion. Their determination to be free of the shackles of traditional religious thought meant that a belief in the re-surrection of the dead could no longer be sustained, and with it went the day of reckoning. Hence the accountability in-herent in the Christian eschatology, by which life here on earth was to be judged, and which could thus serve as a possible method of enforcing certain standards of behaviour during life, was simultaneously jettisoned. In place of the life after death, the 'philosophes' adapted the idea of the prom-ised land here on earth. Hell-fire and damnation, as well as the anticipation of paradise, had lost their regulatory func-tions, and the judgment of the dead—a common feature of many religions, as Brandon has shown—was replaced by the judgment of posterity as the basis of morality. Diderot remarked : 'Posterity is for the philosopher what the other world is for the religious man' ; as Becker himself pointed out, Diderot, of all his contemporaries, was greatly exercised over our relation to posterity, and our desire to be well remembered by those who follow us. Somehow or other, man has to conquer the fear of death and of the unknown that follows it ; it is one of the purposes of mythology to do this, and if the life everlasting is rejected, something must take its place—even if it is the same notion in a different form. For the judgment of the dead, read the judgment of posterity ; for living in the eternal paradise, read living in the eternal memory of posterity.

Diderot came very close to examining the central problem of our responsibility for the way in which we use the world.

Let me quote Becker :

'But if there was no heavenly reward after death, what was
left? Why should any man deny himself? Why suffer
persecution for truth and justice without compensation
here or hereafter? Whatever Diderot's intellect might say,
the good heart of the man assured him that virtue was the
most certain of realities ; and since it was a reality there
must be compensation for the practice of it. The only
compensation Diderot could ever find was the hope of
living for ever in the memory of posterity.'

Even if we believe in the desirability of being judged by
posterity and not being found wanting, we still need to know
why this judgment is important to us. The answer seems to
lie in the way in which we see ourselves in relation to history.
In our attitude towards posterity—our concern for their
welfare, as well as their judgment of our conduct—we are
visualizing ourselves at a certain position along the entire
time-axis of the world, a concept which, obviously enough,
depends on a linear rather than a cyclic view of time. In a
nutshell, our argument runs—as our predecessors were to
us, so should we be to our successors. Such an attitude
requires an effort of objectivity, requiring us to stand away
from the present to overlook all humanity, past, present,
and future, but is easily recognised as arising out of the past
alone. It is, of course, a very old concept and is perhaps something of a historical platitude. Dante began his essay *De
Monarchia* with the following words :

'All men whom the higher Nature has imbued with a love
of truth should feel impelled to work for the benefit of
future generations, whom they will thereby enrich just as
they themselves have been enriched by the labours of
their ancestors. Let there be no doubt in the mind of the
man who has benefitted from the common heritage but

does not trouble to contribute to the common good that he is failing sadly in his duty. For he is not 'a tree beside the running waters bearing fruit in due season', but rather a vicious whirlpool, for ever swallowing things but never throwing them up again'.

In Dante's words we have the notion of our involvement with posterity in the clearest terms; man should repay the debt he owes to his forbears by performing a similar service for those who are to come after him.

At first sight it would appear reasonable to expect that such a view of posterity would be associated with a generally optimistic attitude to life on the earth, but even when the future of the world was in doubt—as, for instance, in Hakewill's *Apologie* which I discussed at the end of the first chapter—it still persisted. A concern for posterity may seem to us to be inconsistent with a belief in the deterioration of the world, but Hakewill could write, in obvious sincerity:

'Let not then the vain shadows of the world's fatal decay keep us either from looking backward to the imitation of our noble predecessors or forward in providing for posterity, but as our predecessors worthily provided for us, so let our posterity bless us in providing for them, it being still as uncertain to us what generations are still to ensue, as it was to our predecessors in their ages'.

Let us be careful, Hakewill seems to be saying; the world may not end just yet, and we would not wish to incur the opprobrium of posterity by abandoning our care for it now. We are grateful to those who looked after it, and handed it on to us in its present state; let us do the same for those that follow after us.

The vision of the individual's position along the dimension of time was particularly well put by J. S. Mill in his book, *Auguste Comte and Positivism*:

'Of that vast unrolling web of human life, the part best known to us is irrevocably past ; this we can no longer serve, but can still love : it comprises for most of us the far greater number of those who have loved us, or from whom we have received benefits, as well as the long series of those who, by their labours and sacrifices for mankind, have deserved to be held in everlasting and grateful remembrance... If we honour as we ought those who have served mankind in the past, we shall feel that we are also working for those benefactors by serving that to which their lives were devoted. And when reflection, guided by history, has taught us the intimacy of the connexion of every age of humanity with every other, making us see in the earthly destiny of mankind the playing out of a great drama, or the action of a prolonged epic, all the generations of man become indissolubly united into a single image, combining all the power over the mind of the idea of Posterity, with our best feelings towards the living world which surrounds us, and towards the predecessors who have made us what we are'.

Mill pays tribute to Comte for the majesty of the 'idea of the general interest of the human race', which 'ascends into the unknown recesses of the past, embraces the manifold present, and descends into the indefinite and unforeseeable future'. What is so significant in this passage from Mill is the vision of all mankind fused into a single humanity, regardless of the position in time at which it was the lot of the individual to find himself placed—past, present, and future all rolled into one.

Is it therefore possible to accept the judgment of posterity as a mediating principle in guiding the way in which we use our dominion over nature? Are we prepared to act in the interests of generations as yet unborn simply because we do

not want them to curse our name for what we have done to
the world? Do we really care *what* posterity is likely to think
of us as individuals? Few of us will be even names to them
(though this is not to deny that the possibility of lasting fame
can be a not inconsiderable spur to human activity). In any
case, the allocation of responsibility for a derelict world is
likely to be placed not so much on us as individuals but on us
all as a generation, conferring on us the comfort of anonymi-
ty. In this respect, at least, the judgment of posterity invokes
less dread than the judgment of God. On this basis, surely,
the verdict of posterity is an unrewarding basis for individual
conduct and the acceptance of sacrifices.

I believe that it is not enough for us merely to argue 'I will
attempt to manage the resources at my disposal in such a way
as to hand them on undiminished to posterity, even though
this involves sacrifices on my part, because it matters a great
deal to me how they judge my conduct in these matters'. This
argument fails to explain *why* we should care either for the
world which posterity will inherit, or for their opinion of
ourselves. It is true that it may provide a valuable pragmatic
approach to the adoption of a useful principle of conduct, a
rule of thumb basis for management, if it can be accepted
uncritically at its face value. Unfortunately it is one of those
notions which begin to dissolve away under critical analysis.
A great deal of the ecological writing on the management of
the earth is patently far too superficial ; the invocation of a
'sacred trust' by which we are held responsible for our
actions, or of an 'ecological conscience' based on the need to
hand over the earth in no worse state than that in which we
found it are both grandiose and high-sounding notions,
emotive clarion-calls to the ideal of conservation, but fail
under critical examination because they are referable only
to the supposed rights of posterity, and we are never told

what these rights are, nor why we should be concerned about them. There is as yet no fully worked-out and satisfying philosophy of conservation, but only a collection of generalities and catch-phrases. These may certainly be useful if not overstretched, but may turn out to be dangerous in that they incorporate their own built-in mechanism for devaluation. If they are rejected as being conceptually unsatisfactory, without anything better being available to take their place, we may be left with a void in which there is no way of restricting further over-exploitation.

It is thus not too much to say that one of the most pressing tasks facing the western world today is to find an acceptable basis for responsible conduct in relation to the natural environment. To attempt to find an answer to the present ecological crisis in terms of more and improved technical intervention is illusory. It may solve this crises, perhaps the next and the few following ones, but it fails to recognize that the situation arises directly from our attitude to the world and what we are to do with it. Improving the *means* of interfering with natural processes may alleviate the worst excesses of our civilization as a temporary measure, but the greater our powers of intervention, the greater the risk of final breakdown. Even if it were possible to stabilize population at or near the present level, our belief in progress, in the continuing improvement of the lot of all mankind, would necessitate increasing domination of the natural environment. We require some basis for restrained conduct which will keep intervention to that level which enables sustained production to continue and to increase, a conceptual position strong enough to counteract our beliefs in domination and increasing population, to avoid the risk of a feed-back of tragic proportions, one which might well destroy western civilization.

A number of ways in which exploitation may be held in

check have been tried in the past, only to be cast aside, perhaps to reappear later in different forms. (As C. S. Lewis has
reminded us, when an old model of the universe is outmoded,
phenomena to support a new one 'will obediently turn up'.)
The early Judaic concept of the sanctity of the property of
the family, with the family conceived of as stretching from
the past through the present into the future, failed under the
stresses and strains of urbanization. The sense of responsibility to God for the use of the earth remained, and could be
used as the basis of a notion of stewardship, in which man is
urged to take a responsible part in the fulfilment of God's
plan for the world. 'Stewardship' would not be expected to
be very efficacious as an abstract ethical principle : to have
the intended effect it needed to be applied to concrete examples such as personal property in resources. Unfortunately it
stood in the way of economic development and, with the
declining hold of Christian discipline, lost any influence it
may ever have had in restraining exploitation. With the
secularization of western world-view came a recrudescence of
the stewardship notion in terms of progress and a duty to
posterity, but mercantile property theory seemed to imply
that what was appropriate to the individual entrepreneur
was, by aggregation, best for society. More recently, we have
seen the development of yet another approach to stewardship, with the state as the authority to which we owe a
responsibility for the management of the resources which
are in our individual care. Evidently western civilization has
always felt the need for a system of allocating responsibility
for the use of the earth, expressed at different times in various
forms, variations on the same theme, consonant with the rest
of the current world-view. These devices for restraint are all
myths, in the scholarly sense, being ways of attempting to
explain or reconcile contradictions and uncertainties. It is,

again, part of our own contemporary mythology that myths have to do only with remote antiquity, but every age has its myths, our own no less than others, and in denying our own reliance on mythology we are only trying to divert our attention from the ways in which we attempt to draw a veil over the realities of our own times. It is assuredly easier for us today to accept as mythological the concept of stewardship in terms of accountability to God, a belief in progress or the rights of posterity, than it is to accept similarly the concept of stewardship seen as responsibility to the state, but that does not make the latest model any less of a myth.

We would also do well to remember that such changes as may have occurred in certain components of our world-view did not necessarily affect the whole of western civilization equally, or at the same time. There are, for instance, sectors of western society which have not repudiated the influence of God in guiding personal conduct, and which still believe in the reality of the last judgment and its overtones of heaven or hell. Similarly there are many people who have not lost their belief in the inevitability and rightness of progress, despite the evidence all around them. There are certainly many others who do not accept the notion of social responsibility, who cannot agree that they owe a duty to society as a whole— although it is implicit in much of present-day thinking and executive action. Different models of the universe exist side-by-side, and remain available, if only in skeletal forms, to be taken to pieces and used as building blocks for a new model. We may now proceed to examine the stock of ideas within the contemporary world-view, to see if there are some which might serve as a solution to our problem, which could be developed to fill the present vacuum. It is at first sight unlikely that any totally new concept could serve this purpose: if such an idea were compatible with our outlook, then it is likely that it is already lurking somewhere in the cultural heritage of our civilization, waiting its turn to be taken up and used to meet a new set of circumstances. However, new inventions provide the possibility of new metaphors, new concepts, so that prediction is dangerous.

One way in which a sense of responsibility for the use of the environment could be inculcated would be a widespread acceptance of the Christian doctrine of stewardship, a belief that we are part of the working out of God's plan for the world, and that we are accountable at the end of the day for the manner in which we have used the resources entrusted to us. There can be no doubt that a return to this view, if it were to be universally accepted, could develop the sense of sacrifice and restraint which is at present lacking. Furthermore, there is in Christianity the long-standing notion that the Fall of Man was accompanied by the Fall of the whole of Nature, that Man's disobedience brought about the downfall of the whole of Creation. It could then fairly be postulated that the deterioration of the environment, which is so plainly visible all around us, is as much part of the divine plan as is the fallen state of man. Yet while the Christian doctrine of salvation is widely accepted as offering *man* a way up from the fallen state, it seems to be frequently overlooked that by the same token the rest of the natural world could be saved along with man, despite the place of this notion in the theology of, for instance, St Paul and St Augustine.

It must however be admitted that the prospect of a religious revival which would enable the doctrine of stewardship to obtain a practical hold over the human use of the earth seems remote. There are both external and internal reasons why this should be so. Firstly, the western attitude to the rest of nature has penetrated deeply into non-western countries, which have modelled their technologies on conceptual sys-

tems alien to their traditional philosophies, and any extension of a notion of stewardship must in some way be seen by
them to be relevant. Secondly, the retreat from Christianity
seems to have gone so far, with much of Christian dogma
apparently discredited, that it is very difficult to see how such
a revival might be brought about. The matter is complicated
by contradictions inherent in the religion itself, as I have
attempted to show. Our world-view has led us to the belief
that the rest of nature was there for man to develop for himself, not just for a stable population in equilibrium with
sustainable resources, but for an ever-growing population.
Modern science and technology have given man such a degree of control over his environment—or so it seems until
some shocking disaster occurs, and for a very short term
thereafter—that he sees no need to postulate a God to whom
he should be responsible. The end result of dissociating himself from the rest of nature has been to dissociate himself
also from the belief in a divine creator. Dominion over his
environment has proceeded so far as to encourage man to
arrogate to himself the role of its creator. If Christianity will
be shown in the end to have failed the world, it will have
failed because it encouraged man to set himself apart from
the rest of nature, or, at the very least, because it failed to
discourage him from doing this. Many of our fundamental
attitudes to the world are seen to have their origin way back
in the early days of western civilization, but simply because
they have been taken for granted they have not been adapted
gradually as circumstances have changed. Consequently, the
ideas that the Christian religion has to offer have been rejected not so much for themselves but because they seem no
longer relevant. Hence it seems to me that though a revival of
interest in religion would indeed be able to set western man
on a new path, it would have to be either a new religion or

some transformation of Judeo-Christian tenets more suited to the age. Its first task would be the establishment of a new integration of man with the rest of nature.

It has also become fashionable to pit science against religion, with the intention of blaming science-without-religion for the ills of the contemporary world. This is one of the most widespread and ignorant of the myths of today, and it must be refuted at once. It has arisen because the various strands of thought in western culture have been separated out, and in the process of separation they have been placed in opposition. A world-view is a world-view *in its totality*, not a job-lot of isolated components, and separating religion and science in the western world-view fails to recognize the essential part the religious elements have played in providing the necessary framework within which science was able to develop. Dominion over nature demands the separation of man from nature, and is an essential concept of the Judeo-Christian outlook. Berdyaev possibly overstated the case by neglecting the development of science in other religions when he wrote in *The Meaning of History* :

> 'However paradoxical it may seem, I am convinced that Christianity alone made possible both positive science and technique. As long as man had found himself in communion with nature and had based his life upon mythology, he could not raise himself above nature through an act of apprehension by means of the natural sciences or technique... When immersed in nature and communing with its inner life, man could neither apprehend it scientifically nor master it technically.'

This is not perhaps the place to enlarge on the importance of Judeo-Christian (that is, non-Greek) elements in the western science of nature, but the important point is that it is just not possible to blame *either* religion *or* science for what has been called 'The Rape of the Earth'. Both are important and interacting components of our outlook, and our overall outlook has to change if our management of the earth is to alter.

For much the same reasons, Nasr's plea to the West to develop a metaphysic which would re-establish a sacred quality in nature is unlikely to succeed, simply because an approach based on harmony between man and nature is incompatible with the rest of western world-view. This is not to suggest that such a harmony with nature could not be achieved, even widely accepted, but it would involve the wholesale jettisoning of many cherished western attitudes — particularly those stressing man's control of nature, on which the development of modern science has rested. It would not therefore be sufficient to examine Christian theology, as he suggests, in order to find a way of developing or grafting on a new or newly-revived sense of harmony with nature. To replace 'dominion over nature' by 'harmony with nature' would be to remove from western civilization its most significant attribute, and would involve its replacement by another, albeit perhaps a better, civilization.

It seems to me that almost the only course open to western man is based on the vision of all mankind stretched out along the dimension of time. As a general rule, most of us are prepared so to manage our affairs that we and our contemporaries do not suffer; self-interest sees to that. It is the transfer of this interest in the general good of mankind to the future — particularly the remote future — that raises difficulties. By expanding our view of the general good of mankind, by redefining 'mankind' in terms of the whole of humanity, dead, living or as yet unborn, we may perhaps be able to assess what we do in terms of the good of mankind, regardless of the position of the individual along the time axis of the world. This would take as its basis Mill's 'all generations indissolu-

bly united into a single image'. The merging of all humanity
would at least provide us with a reason for enlightened conduct in the management of the world, since it leads easily
enough into a concern for the greatest good for the greatest
number of people. To quote Bury's *The Idea of Progress*,
'The ethical end may still be formulated, with the Utilitarians, as the greatest happiness of the greatest number ; only
the greatest number includes, as Kidd observed, "the members of generations yet unborn or unthought of"'.

I do not know whether such a vision of humanity in its
totality could become part of western world-view, though it
does not seem to raise particular problems of compatibility.
It does however involve a re-examination of our timescales,
and of all western values the linear concept of time seems
the most firmly fixed and thus least open to change. Does the
vision of indissoluble unity of mankind imply a contraction
or an expansion in our time scale? At first sight, we may seem
to be asking a man to contract his view of past, present, and
future to a single point in time, visualizing all mankind as
existing in some way simultaneously, an attitude quite
foreign to our accepted concepts of time and history. Alternatively, we might approach this vision rather as an expansion of the present, an instant of time always difficult to
envisage. We are accustomed to use our notion of the present
in a distinctly relative fashion, covering such a period of time
as may be appropriate to our context. The strict present, the
interface between the past and the future, disappears on
analysis, as we admit when we speak of 'the present time',
'the present day', even 'the present century'. We should perhaps envisage the unity of mankind as stretching the present
rather than as contracting past and future to a single point in
time, but even in this way it probably involves too radical a
change in traditional attitudes to gain general acceptance.

9

The World of the Future

I began this book by examining the claims that we were living through a period often referred to as an 'ecological crisis'. Despite suggestions that western civilization has experienced previous periods of ecological disruption, and although the present situation was forecast with remarkable percipience and clarity by George Marsh in his influential book *Man and Nature*, first published over one hundred years ago, there exists today this unmistakable feeling of an unexpected, and even undeserved, 'crisis'. To some extent this is probably due to a contemporary penchant for an age of crises, as distinct from mere transitions, but I want to turn now to the significance of the word 'crisis' in this context, and then to project my findings to the future world of man.

The purpose of this book has been to examine the development of those ideas which have led to the designation of the present place of man in nature as an 'ecological crisis'. I have argued that man's belief in his absolute right to dominate the rest of nature, and in the propriety of an ever-increasing human population, coupled with a failure to elaborate a concept of responsibility which would hold the situation in check, have brought us to the position in which we find our-

selves today, when the only remedy for the misuse of techniques for the management of nature is the adoption of
further and more advanced techniques. This situation, which
I have earlier referred to as 'tail-chasing', militates against
the adoption of other philosophies of resource management.
An alternative argument could be put forward, that the belief
in man's right to dominion over the rest of nature cannot
itself be held *responsible* for the present situation in the way
I have suggested ; that, faced with an ever-expanding population, at first on a purely local scale, the origins of which are to
be found quite simply in the reproductive biology of man as
a species, the increasing pressure of population on the available resources acted as sufficient spur to improved technical
control over the means of production. The rest followed from
this, so that the strongly held concept of dominion over
nature arose post hoc *and* propter hoc. There is undoubtedly
much truth in this, and it would indeed be surprising if a
notion of dominion did not arise alongside, and develop with,
an increasing ability to control the resources of the environment. Nevertheless, this argument fails to take into account
that human societies seem to feel a need to elaborate a justification — or at least a rationalization — of their actions, and
the resulting beliefs become both an explanation of the past
and a model for the present and the future. Indeed, these
beliefs become so fixed in our thinking that as time goes by it
becomes increasingly difficult to contemplate a form of conduct which departs radically from them. Even though we
may be all too well aware of the implications of the ideational
framework of contemporary resource management, we
seem unable to alter our basic approach. The importance of
our inherited concepts of dominion and responsibility therefore lies not so much in their explanation of the past but in the
way in which they mould our present and our future conduct.

But why should we be experiencing a sense of *crisis*? The situation is not new ; it has been building up slowly over the centuries, and the evidence for it has long been available, though it will readily be admitted that the pace of technical intervention in natural processes has greatly accelerated in recent decades, and that many more people are now brought into contact with it. It seems scarcely possible that despite the mass of evidence, and all that poets, artists and others have done to draw attention to their fears for the future of the world, the awareness of ecological degeneration can only just now have burst in upon popular imagination. I suspect that there have always been artists and writers of a sensitivity sufficient to understand the implications of man's dominion over nature, and who have attempted to project their concern to their contemporaries. Unfortunately, such warnings are easily brushed on one side, and the propounders dismissed as unpractical visionaries, in the comfortable atmosphere that the unwillingness to face reality always seems to engender. This refusal to face or to discuss the unpleasant has, I believe, worse consequences than the individual greed or selfishness which operate as the more immediate causes of the adoption and continued use of unsuitable technology since these will, in the event, automatically adjust themselves, though not necessarily in the most appropriate way, to changing circumstances. Given that the situation has been growing progressively worse, despite the many warnings over the centuries, it is at first sight surprising that its impact on popular feeling should have come so quickly, and that it should have come under the scare-banner of crisis, with its doom-ridden, apocalyptic message of Beware, for the end of the world is at hand.

I believe that the answer lies in our attitude to states of crisis. By this I do not wish to suggest that the word 'crisis' has itself become devalued by familiarity arising from over-use, in the same way as have such words as 'awful' or 'terri-ble'. I think that we should recognize that a sense of crisis is an important component of contemporary mythology, that we believe ourselves to be living in a time at which there is some unique feature in the relationship between the past and the future, and that this feature has so impressed itself on our imagination that we examine all our current problems against it. Thus any difficulty facing our society is seen in terms of this peculiar 'end of an era' feeling, so that, regardless of similar situations which we may be aware of as having existed in the past, *our* problems are always more serious, more acute, more eruptive. Looking back over the past from our vantage-point in the present, we can observe the develop-ment of trends or the evolution of doctrines and models of the universe, and we label those moments when change seems to us to be most rapid as periods of transition ; the further we get from them—or rather, the further they are removed in time from ourselves—the smoother the transi-tions seem to be. But we are living, or so we inform ourselves, not in a time of transition, but in a time of crisis. To introduce this sense of crisis into the present relationship between man and his environment seems to me both short-sighted and dangerous, for several reasons. First, a notion of crisis, by its very nature, diverts attention from the steady and gradual build-up of the factors which have contributed to the now evident state of deterioration, and hence obscures the reasons by which it has come about, from which we could deduce a sensible policy for the future. Secondly, it brings us face to face with what purports to be a new and, hence, a uniquely disturbing phenomenon, for which we may not see ourselves to blame. We may feel that we do not have the necessary conceptual or technological framework to deal with the situation, leading to attitudes which are conducive to a state of pessimism in which little is likely to be done. Thirdly, crises, like prophecies, seem to me to run the risk of imposing their own pattern on the future, by suggesting a likelihood of change in a particular direction — in other words, postulate a crisis and a predictable reaction to that crisis will be provoked.

The whole of the analysis to which this book has been devoted has indicated that the present ecological situation has nothing of the 'crisis' about it ; there is no suggestion of suddenness, or imminence of some decisive, let alone catastrophic, change, either for better or worse (though we only seem to invoke the word 'crisis' when the anticipated change is for the worse). It is a condition which has developed slowly, and future changes are likely to remain gradual, though perhaps occurring rather less gradually than previously. The undeniable increase in the rate of technological intervention may be expected to continue, but this does not constitute a crisis, but rather a state of continuous transition. There is certainly no evidence that the end of the world is at hand, and even the approach of the year 2000 has so far evoked little in the way of millenarian forebodings such as greeted the year 1000. I would suggest that our obsession with an ecological crisis reflects another facet of what I may call the contemporary myth of comfort, since it implies that once the crisis is over and done with, a new situation will arise which can be allowed to run its course without unreasonable change (until, perhaps, another crisis blows up). The reality is, of course, decisively less comfortable, since it is that we are living in a time of rapid and continuous transition, and that the future, instead of being more secure, more stable, is likely to become increasingly unstable and susceptible to more frequent and more violent changes and oscillations. Hence the need for a myth of crisis, the assumption of calm waters beyond the storm, a period of security in which people can live-out their lives as they plan. The myth is socially necessary, since there are few people who can face the reality of continuous change with equanimity.

If we can thus rid ourselves of this sense of crisis, recognizing that we should rather look forward to a period of continuous and even violent change, we find ourselves able to proceed to a projection into the future of the trends which have shaped the present. We have noted that the present situation came about by a gradual intensification of control of nature under the stimulus of continuing increases in the pressure of population on resources, within a world-view that has stressed—perhaps as a result of the very development of those techniques—that man has a right to set himself apart from the rest of nature. A number of possible ways of imbuing a sense of responsibility for the management of the environment have been proposed and discussed, but gave very little ground for optimism.

I think it would generally be agreed that, given improvements in political and economic communication, it should be possible to begin to eliminate some of the existing pockets of starvation. It would also be agreed that by the adoption of the best available methods of resource management—under which heading should be included the provision of water, forest products, recreation, amenity, and energy supplies as well as food ; and by the spread of intensive technological management to more and more of the earth's surface, the world's food production should be able to keep ahead of increasing population. But for how long? The usual term used in this connection is the 'foreseeable' future. Probably no two people would agree on what the word 'foreseeable' means to them ; most people would use the term to cover their own lifetime, or until the end of the present century, or for the next fifty years or so. I consider that this is a ridiculously short period to be concerned for the future of the human race, and that we should be thinking in terms of periods of at least 250 or 500 years if we are to make any progress in rational use of the world's resources. It is, of course, extremely difficult to visualize a time-scale of this magnitude, and we cannot now know what advances in technology will occur, nor in which direction they will lead us, but unless we plan on a long-term basis we are unlikely to get initial priorities right.

Seen in this perspective, the spectre of the Malthusian situation begins to haunt us again. Given the increases in world population implied by a time-scale of these dimensions, the possibility of sufficient food and water being made available cannot but be once more in doubt, unless we are prepared to proceed in the blind faith that 'science will provide'. Since Malthus wrote, nearly 200 years ago, we have been successful in extending the limiting values by increasing food supplies and decreasing disease, so that the onset of the checks has been delayed, but the blunt fact remains that man can only increase in population to the numbers for which food can be available, even assuming perfect control of technology and distribution. To believe otherwise is to live in a fool's paradise. The Malthusian argument that population will increase at a high rate until it comes up against natural limitations is—with one important reservation to which I must shortly return—undeniable, and is supported by widespread ecological studies of the population dynamics of many species, in that an equilibrium between population and resources is achieved by the production of excess individuals, thinned out by starvation, predation or disease, frequently before they can reach the age at which reproductive activity begins.

Malthus himself believed that the natural limitation of population size was imminent, but arguments aimed at falsifying his analysis by pointing to the failure of his dismal prophecies seem to me to be dangerous and ill-informed. In the first place, it is quite wrong-headed to discuss the relationship between population and food supplies on a world-wide basis, using total world population and potential food production, since this assumes a perfect movement of both people and food over the surface of the earth. This does not accord with reality, which is that the world is divided into discrete regions, with very much less than perfect adjustment between them, and it is *within* these regions that the Malthusian situation should be examined. If the examination is restricted to western civilization, it is doubtless a fair summary to say that food production has, by and large, kept ahead of population, though only by drawing on the resources of the rest of the world. It would be utterly wrong to say that the same is true of all the developing countries of the 'third world'. In countries such as India, there remain continuous or spasmodic pockets of starvation which either retard the population growth or render human existence miserable, and areas where disease regularly takes its toll of human life. This situation has been discussed by C. G. Darwin in terms of the 'starving margin', whereby, regardless of an overall increase in world population or improvements in food supply, there may always be expected to be people, somewhere, living under conditions of starvation. An increase in world population may indeed be accompanied by an increase in the number of people living in starvation conditions at the 'starving margin'. Even if a stable world population could be achieved, in equilibrium with food production, this situation of the starving margin could only be averted if the distribution of food supplies could be made perfect. At a time when effective world government—either at the political or the socio-economic level—begins to look increasingly remote, and when regional and national self-sufficiency seems to be hardening, the prospect of improvements in the distribution of food supplies to the starving margin can scarcely be held to be encouraging.

I have just referred to an important reservation in the operation of a Malthusian argument ; this reservation concerns the attainment of a stable population. Malthus' argument was centred on the assumption of an unrestricted increase in population, though he recognized that by such means as delayed marriage a check on the rate of increment could be achieved. His analysis breaks down if a controlled world population growth could be obtained by means other than the limitations placed on it by natural factors such as starvation, disease or predation. Much of the recent discussion on the ecological 'crisis' revolves around this question of how to control population numbers, it being assumed, usually tacitly, that food production cannot expand sufficiently, or sufficiently quickly, to keep abreast of the population 'explosion'. Whether or not this is true depends in large measure on the time-scale involved, though this is rarely mentioned. This debate is tangled up with another argument, to which I shall return, that the necessary expansion of food production would involve unacceptable changes in the environment. Lacking a full and detailed understanding of the magnitude of the problems of increasing food production, and failing to face up to the implications of the acceptability, or unacceptability, of changes in the environment, attention is diverted to the remaining factor in the Malthusian equation, the prospect of a continuing population increase.

Although many of the problems concerned in the attainment of a controlled population growth have been widely discussed and subjected to detailed study, there remain some aspects which seem to be rarely recognized. If a programme of stabilized population growth is to be satisfactory, it must be a world-wide programme ; if it is not, immigration and emigration will undo much of the benefit, unless these are strictly controlled. There are, of course, indications in many parts of the world that the realization of a need to control population movement is growing, and that restrictions on movement must be accepted if existing standards of living are not to be threatened, but this awareness is based as a rule on selfish considerations of holding on to what has been achieved, rather than on the basis of rational world population postulates. Unfortunately this realization is readily confused by racialist overtones, since inevitably population movement is preponderantly towards the richer countries, which tend to be of one colour, from the poorer, which are of another. The experience of the United States of America, amongst other countries, shows that barriers to the movement of population may not necessarily be located at points of entry, but may occur *within* a country by the operation of socio-economic factors which are all the more insidious by being covert. It follows that if a policy of controlled population increase is to be adopted, it must either be designed and executed in such a way as to apply to the whole world equally, or be accompanied by a restriction of freedom of movement, which would otherwise set much of the advantage at naught.

The operation of such a policy on a world-wide basis would itself create many problems, the most important being the identity of the organization on which would devolve the duty of establishing the proper overall size of world population and, even more difficult to determine, the proportion of the total allowable in individual countries. If this could be achieved, there still remains the question of policing the regulations, because the problems of census — let alone those of obtaining the agreement and co-operation of individual governments — might well prove to be greatest in the very countries in which regulation was most desirable. Before any policy of deliberate population control could be implemented, it would be necessary to obtain general and world-wide agreement that it was desirable *in principle*, regardless of the level of population that might subsequently be set. At the present time it would almost certainly be impossible to obtain such agreement, though the difficulties might ease in the future with changes in the climate of opinion and in the evolution of genuinely supra-national world organizations that would include *all* the countries of the world. There are, of course, countries which would still be able to look forward to considerable increases in population, just as there are some — including, probably, Great Britain — in which a planned reduction might well be recommended. The attitude of mind which holds that it is right and proper that the population of the world should increase — that when God said, 'Be fruitful and multiply and replenish the world', He really meant what He was saying — embodies one of the most strongly-held and deeply-felt of all the western convictions, and may, indeed, intensify under pressure, insisting that population control is a matter for the rest of the world only. It is possible that the countries of western civilization might agree on a sensible programme of population restriction, if only to safeguard their high standards of living, accompanied, as would be necessary, by limits on immigration, but it would be difficult, if not impossible, to maintain such a policy in the face of rapidly increasing numbers in the rest of the world. In this situation the operative mechanism for the control of population might easily move from starvation to predation. It seems to me that the evolution of suitable means of world government is an essential prerequisite to the development of a population policy which might have any hope of success.

Given the desire and the intention to stabilize world population, there remains for discussion the way in which this is to be achieved. Since the number of people living on the earth at any one time depends on the relationship between birth-rates and death-rates, control can obviously be directed either towards decreasing birthrates or increasing death-rates. The second possibility, equally obviously, is unlikely to obtain much serious support in a world that retains any belief in the sanctity of human life (though this belief may perhaps become attenuated in a situation of population 'crisis'), so that attention is concentrated on the control of birth-rates. Birth control could come about in two ways, voluntarily or involuntarily. The first category includes dependence on such methods as financial inducements through grants or taxes ; increased education and facilities for contraception, given the research needed to improve the efficiency of such procedures to a point at which their reliability can be guaranteed ; and the liberalization of abortion practices. Infanticide can be ruled out on the grounds that it is a device for increasing death-rates, not controlling birth-rates, and is hence unlikely to gain widespread popularity, but it must not be forgotten that abortion can also be held to come within this same category. Certain methods of contraception, though not necessarily the concept of birth regulation *per se*, are similarly unacceptable to some sections of the population on religious grounds, though, I believe, to a declining extent. Unless such objections could be overcome, a policy of strict population regulation depending on voluntary co-operation could hardly be envisaged in the first place. To be effective,

voluntary population restriction would have to command
absolute agreement throughout society, and in all parts of
the world, regardless of differences in world-view, and seems
to me to be unlikely to give the necessary degree of control.

On the other hand, involuntary control of population
growth by the adoption of what is in effect the licensing of
births would undoubtedly be a much more certain way of
regulating world population, though at the moment such a
concept would seem to be wholly unacceptable. Technically,
it may well become possible to achieve temporary steriliza-
tion, removable at will—perhaps with the presentation of a
licence to bear a child—but the administrative problems of
operating such a scheme would be formidable, particularly
in the face of opposition. There is no doubt that the evolution
of the powers of the modern state, and the myth of the responsibility owed to it by the individual, makes the enforced
control of reproduction a possible—though to us a night-
marish, even utterly improper—suggestion, but it is nevertheless the direction in which social planning may evolve.
Because we reject such a possibility today does not mean that
it will be equally unpalatable to the society of, let us say, 250
years hence. We may think that the very idea of queuing at
the Town Hall for a 'Birth-Licence' for a new baby is both
repugnant and ridiculous, but so would the possibilities and
administrative problems of organ transplantation have appeared to the society of a century or two ago. The long time-
span within which I have been arguing may be found to give
the lie to many of our most cherished convictions.

The problem of strict population control is, in any case, a
long-term one, and in the short term there is little doubt that
it would be technically possible to support a vastly increased
population—Clark estimates 47 billion people on an Ameri-
can-type diet or 157 billion on a Japanese-type diet. Future

research and development are likely to increase rather than to decrease these estimates. Nevertheless, arguments that are based on simple relationships between potential calorific and protein production and per capita dietary intake conveniently overlook a number of difficulties. First of all, they demand that the entire agricultural area of the world be brought up to the highest standards of technical and managerial efficiency, although this would involve radical and far-reaching changes in rural sociology, particularly in systems of land tenure and the deployment of capital and labour resources. Secondly, they assume a perfect mechanism for the distribution of food surpluses, and the elaboration of the political and economic framework within which this could take place. Thirdly, they require the elimination of much of the present waste in storage, transportation, processing, in the kitchen and at the table. Fourthly, they ignore factors other than food which may operate to limit the growth of population, and it may well be that, in the long run, water and not food turns out to be the important limiting resource. Even though it may be some long time before the socio-economic difficulties are solved, the continued improvement in agricultural technology and practice coupled with increasing willingness, in some countries at least, to set voluntary limits to the number of births may be expected to ensure that the population of the world will continue to increase. Why then should there be this sense of an ecological 'crisis'?

The essential problem lies not in the provision of so much additional food and other natural resource products, but in the changes in the environment which would inevitably accompany it. If agricultural production is to be expanded continuously to provide ever-increasing supplies of food, the environment must be progressively simplified ; the danger lies in this simplification and its attendant risks of oscillation and breakdown. Simplification itself is easily enough recognized, though the symptoms of breakdown may be less well known, and simplification may involve unpredictable or as yet unsuspected dangers. It is essential for us to keep a sense of proportion when considering the effects of technology on the environment, and the whole history of resource management, from the least sophisticated hunting and gathering systems to present-day advanced technical agriculture, has involved progressive simplification of the environment, increasing attempts to return the natural ecosystem to early stages of succession. It is the balance between the demands for production and the demands for stability that is now in question ; man must eat, and if this requires a further simplification of the environment, the possible loss of stability and the increased risk of breakdowns are just part of the price which may have to be paid for it.

The present disquiet in western civilization arises not so much from an awareness of a risk of starvation but from watching the environment deteriorate and facing the disasters which the breakdown of ecological homeostasis brings in its train. We should remind ourselves that we are viewing the world from a position of privilege, that the problems of western civilization are not necessarily those of the rest of the world, and that it is one thing to complain about pollution and loss of scenic amenity on a full stomach, quite another to be faced with an ever-present risk of starvation. Demands for a high degree of scenic amenity and for the conservation of a wide range of environmental resources are luxuries appertaining to advanced technological societies ; so, too, in the main, the problems of pollution are those of advanced societies, though modern methods of communication have ensured that they spill over to the rest of the world. The dichotomy in our approach to our natural surroundings is neatly mirrored in the increasing adoption of technically sophisticated agricultural processes such as 'factory farming', which might be expected on first sight to be welcome in that they release large areas of agricultural land for non-agricultural purposes such as amenity or recreation, and may well lessen fears of further deterioration. However, they are opposed by arguments of sentiment, on the grounds that animals are being subjected to conditions in which they should not be allowed to live ; sentiment is, of course, a perfectly proper basis for argument as long as we are quite clear what we are doing. Some people are apt to cite such processes as 'inhuman', an adjective which, when employed in this context, speaks for itself. Since farming methods such as these are likely to grow, being typical examples of the trends towards simplification, it is not difficult to envisage a system in which, in the course of time, most food production is carried out in factories on the fringes of large conurbations, employing techniques as yet in the laboratory and experimental stages, leaving the countryside free for other purposes such as watergathering or public health. Although this may now seem no more than a dream or a nightmare, depending on how you look at it, it is a logical extension of existing tendencies towards increased technical control, centralized planning, greater leisure opportunities and the insistence on cheaper food, though not necessarily food of higher quality.

The cause of the widespread and very real concern, as I see it, is that the increased technical control of natural processes is seen to bring about, firstly, greatly increased simplification of the human environment and, secondly, a loss of ecological homeostasis ; the first leads to an unacceptable reduction in the quality of our surroundings, the second to a greater risk of 'technological disasters'. How are these fears to be met?

Taking the second one first, for it is, I believe, of subsidiary importance, the incidence of technical disasters can presumably be reduced by improved administrative procedures, though the unpredictable elements of human error and lack of judgment will always be liable to break through any control system, however sophisticated and free from loopholes it may appear to be. Indeed, the more effective the control systems which can be devised, the more serious will be those disasters which nevertheless slip through the net. It is highly improbable, to say the least, that technical manipulation of natural processes at the level needed can be so safeguarded that the risk of occasional breakdowns can be entirely eliminated, particularly so long as economic incentives tempt people to disregard agreed regulations. Furthermore, the natural arrogance of man and the confidence he places in the systems he has himself created may be expected to cause him to minimize the risks involved, and subsequently to excuse the disasters once they have occurred. It is unlikely that even a detailed understanding of the risks of ecological disruption will provide a mechanism for controlling the worst excesses of manipulative intervention in natural processes, and the fear of breakdowns will, I suspect, always be with us, and may be expected to increase rather than decrease.

The other and more immediately apparent cause for concern is the decline in the *quality* of the human environment. I have earlier remarked that this concern seems to be particularly associated with the privileged, well-fed western society, and it is certainly true that the great upsurge in demands for conservation, for the maintenance of ecological diversity and the elimination of the visually undesirable have come from these countries, not those for whom a bird in the hand really is better than two in the bush. It is equally true that it is the technically advanced countries that have at their disposal the most powerful means of despoiling their own surroundings. It does not follow from this that people brought up in subsistence agricultural or even simpler systems of resource management are unaware of the environment in which they live ; indeed they have to maintain a much more intimate relation with it, for survival depends on accuracy of observation and the deployment of accumulated folk-knowledge of nature. It is a strange paradox that the societies with the leisure and position to protest most loudly about the deterioration of the environment should also be those in which the vast majority of the people have become urbanized, have lost the art of observing nature, and are very largely unaware of the extent of their dependence on their natural resources. The answer seems to be that even within such societies concern for the environment is confined to a small minority, albeit a well-informed and highly articulate minority.

Concern for the quality of the environment is not simply a question of aesthetics, but contains elements of reproach also ; a grossly polluted river, for instance, is both an affront to our aesthetic sensibilities and evidence of a technical breakdown, just as the elimination of wildlife by the use of persistent pesticides offends our sense of the place of animals in nature as well as drawing attention to the use of a method of ecological simplification adopted either in ignorance of its far-reaching effects or as a result of economic expediency. However difficult it may be to separate these two attitudes, we would recognize that we *are* concerned about quality, but also that it is right and proper that we *should* be. Our attitude to the human environment is inevitably determined by our recollections of the surroundings in which we ourselves grew up (how many books on conservation begin with the expression of such a sentiment as 'When I was a boy, you could find fifty different species of birds in the fields

beyond our back fence ; now there are only five'?). Added to
our own recollections is, perhaps, a romanticized idea of the
world which more fortunate people are believed to inhabit,
all adding up to an ideal world in which we ourselves would
like to live. When we find ourselves confronted with an
environment which increasingly fails to match up to our
expectations, we protest, not only for ourselves but for
posterity as well. This is all very natural, and it is, indeed,
greatly to our credit that we are prepared to go to considerable lengths to defend our idealized environment from the
insidious deterioration that we find on all sides, but it fails to
take into account the way in which the human environment
has always been changing, though admittedly at an increasing pace, throughout the development of our civilization. From our own vantage point in history, we project our
own ideals and our standards into the future, believing that
those elements of our environment which we hold most pre-
cious will also appear so to our own descendents.

Where we are aware of changes in our environment that
are potentially dangerous to our own survival, such as the
accumulation in human tissue of radio-active compounds or
pesticide residues, we are right to draw attention to them in
the most urgent terms, knowing as we do that such changes
operate so quickly as to outstrip any evolutionary development in human metabolism which might arise to contain
them. It is quite another matter when we are concerned with
the preservation of less tangible aspects of aesthetic quality
in our surroundings. Probably no generation would have
viewed with pleasure the environment of, say, a century
ahead, though we must be careful to qualify such a statement
by identifying just who it is that we are concerned with. The
farmer or squire of the middle of the last century would
probably have been appalled if he could have foreseen the

changes which would be wrought in the English countryside over only three or four generations, and the effects these would have upon his daily way of life, but the agricultural labourer of those days might well have viewed the same changes as a step nearer Paradise. We should be careful not to judge the future with the eyes of the present, but these are the only eyes we have, and we have only our own emotional response to our environment to depend on. We are faced with choosing between assuming that our descendents will share our own aesthetic susceptibilities, or neglecting their interests altogether ; we cannot forecast what they will demand of their environment. Inevitably, the increasing world population and the consequent changes in the environment will mean that posterity will inhabit a totally different world, and it is probable that when the time comes most people, as now, will be concerned about changes and will seek, as we do, to hold on to an ideal world and to preserve it for posterity. Changes come relatively slowly, and man adapts himself and his style of living to the world in which he finds himself. The idea that man's mastery over nature is so complete that he can create for himself the very environment he wants is a dangerous illusion and a pathetic myth, designed to conceal the discomforting reality that while man can undoubtedly change the environment almost beyond recognition, it may well turn out not to measure up to his expectations. In the event, having changed the environment, man proceeds to adapt his own way of life to the new circumstances.

This is not to suggest that all the changes we make in our environment are for the worse ; many are for the better, as shown by the steadily increasing expectation of life. It is a matter of proportion, and if we are to continue to feed an expanding population, some changes consequent upon this are sure to be unpleasant and must be recognized for what they are. Nor does it mean that progress is illusory, that no matter how hard we strive we cannot move towards a better world. While we may hope that we can leave the world a better place than we found it, we cannot guarantee in which direction the changes which we may set in motion will go, nor how they may be viewed by those who come after us. As I have repeatedly emphasised, western civilization leans heavily on such concepts as the right of man to dominion over the rest of nature and a continuing increase in world population. These concepts were long ago set on a collision course, and we cannot say for how long the collision can be avoided. If western civilization has failed, it has failed because it has been unable to find a concept which would engender a feeling of responsibility for the use to which we put our control over nature, and at this late stage it is not easy to suggest one which would be compatible with the rest of our world-view. We have no means of knowing if, faced with far-reaching, even revolutionary changes in our environment, our fundamental approach to the world will change to allow a more stable relationship between man and nature within the framework of our existing society or whether western civilization itself will have to be replaced. It is not easy to forecast where the building blocks for a new model of the universe will be discovered.

Acknowledgments

I have drawn freely from the books listed in the bibliography, and to their authors and publishers I express, personally and on behalf of the Edinburgh University Press, my grateful acknowledgment of this essential liberty of quotation. To the following I am specially indebted for the more extensive excerpts in my text: *Allen and Unwin* (S. H. Nasr, The Encounter of Man and Nature; P. Self and H. J. Storing, The State and the Farmer); *Athlone Press* (K. Cragg, The Privilege of Man); *Blackwell* (Aquinas, Selected Political Writings, ed. D'Entrèves, trans. Dawson); *Geoffrey Bles* (N. Berdyaev, The Meaning of History, trans. Reavey); *Frank Cass* (V. Harris, All Coherence Gone); *Cornell University Press* (R. Redfield, The Primitive World and its Transformation); *Macmillan*, New York (F. S. C. Northrop, The Meeting of East and West); *Oliver and Boyd* (V. C. Wynne-Edwards, Animal Dispersion in Relation to Social Behaviour); *Oxford University Press* (J. Baillie, The Belief in Progress; L. White, Medieval Technology and Social Change); *Yale University Press* (C. L. Becker, The Heavenly City of the Eighteenth-Century Philosophers).

J.B.

Bibliography

Altmann, A. (1968) Homo Imago Dei in Jewish and Christian theology. *J. Relig.* 48, 235

Aquinas (1965) (ed. D'Entrèves, trans. Dawson) *Selected Political Writings.* Oxford : Blackwell

Bacon, F. (1960) (ed. Anderson) *The New Organon and Related Writings.* Indianapolis : Bobbs-Merill

Baillie, J. (1950) *The Belief in Progress.* London : O. U. P.

Barr, J. (1962) *Biblical Words for Time.* London : S. C. M.

Becker, C. L. (1932) *The Heavenly City of the Eighteenth-Century Philosphers.* New Haven : Yale

Berdyaev, N. (1936) (trans. Reavey) *The Meaning of History.* London : Bles

Berelson, B. (1969) Beyond family planning. *Science* 163, 533

Boorstin, D. J. (1948) *The Lost World of Thomas Jefferson.* New York : Holt

Boserup, E. (1965) *The Conditions of Agricultural Growth.* London : Allen and Unwin

Bradfield, W. (1909) The social teaching of the early christian fathers. In (ed. Keeble) *The Social Teaching of the Bible,* p. 249. London : Culley

Braidwood, R. J. and C. A. Reed (1957) The achievement and early consequences of food production : a consideration of the archaeological and natural-historical evidence. *Cold Spring Harbour Symp. Quant. Biol.* 22, 19

Brandon, S.G.F. (1963) *Creation Legends of the Ancient Near East*. London : Hodder and Stoughton

Brandon, S.G.F. (1967) *The Judgement of the Dead*. London : Weidenfeld and Nicholson

Bury, J.B. (1920) *The Idea of Progress*. London : Macmillan

Carr Saunders, A.M. (1922) *The Population Problem*. Oxford : Clarendon Press

Cassuto, U. (1961) (trans. Abrahams) *A Commentary on the Book of Genesis. Part 1, From Adam to Noah*. Jerusalem : Magnes

Chamberlayne, J.H. (1966) *Man In Society*. London : Epworth Press

Childs, B.S. (1960) *Myth and Reality in the Old Testament*. London : S.C.M.

Clark, C. (1967) *Population Growth and Land Use*. London : Macmillan

Clark, C. and M.R. Haswell (1967) *The Economics of Subsistence Agriculture*. (3rd Edition) London : Macmillan

Collumella, (1941) (trans. Ash) *De Re Rustica*. London : Loeb

Comte, A. (1911) (trans. Hutton) *Early Essays in Social Philosophy*. London : Routledge

Condorcet, A.N. de (1955) (trans. Barraclough) *Sketch for a Historical Picture of the Progress of the Human Mind*. London : Weidenfeld and Nicholson

Cragg, K. (1965) *Counsels in Contemporary Islam*. Edinburgh : Edinburgh University Press

Cragg, K. (1968) *The Privilege of Man*. London : Athlone Press

Cumberland, K.B. (1962) Moas and men : New Zealand about A D 1250. *Geogr. Rev.* 52, 151

Dante Aligheri (1954) (ed. Nicholl) *Monarchy and Three Political Letters*. London : Weidenfeld and Nicholson

Darling, F.F. (1955) *West Highland Survey*. London : O.U.P

Darwin, C.G. (1952) *The Next Million Years*. London : Hart-Davis

Devereux, G. (1960) *A Study of Abortion in Primitive Societies*. London : Yoseloff

Douglas, M. (1967) The meaning of myth, with special reference to 'La Geste d'Asdiwal.' In (ed. Leach) *The Structural Study of Myth and Totemism*, p.49. London : Tavistock

Driver, S.R. (1909) *The Book of Genesis*. (7th Ed.) London : Methuen

Dubos, R. (1965) *Man Adapting*. New Haven : Yale

Elton, C.E. (1958) *The Ecology of Invasions by Animals and Plants*. London : Methuen

Evans, J.M. (1968) *Paradise Lost and the Genesis Tradition*. Oxford : Clarendon Press

Evelyn, J. (1933) (ed. Macaulay) *Fumifugium* : *or the Inconvenience of the Air and Smoake of London Dissipated*. London : National Smoke Abatement Society

Fagley, R.M. (1960) *The Population Explosion and Christian Responsibility*. New York : O.U.P.

Firth, R. (1939) *Primitive Polynesian Economy*. London : Routledge

Frankfort, H. and H.A., J.A.Wilson, T.Jacobsen and W.A. Irwin. (1946) *The Intellectual Adventure of Ancient Man*. Chicago : Chicago University Press

Gellner, E. (1964) *Thought and Change*. London : Weidenfeld and Nicolson

Grace, F. (1953) *The Concept of Property in Modern Christian Thought*. Urbana : University of Illinois Press

Graham, E.H. (1944) *Natural Principles of Land Use*. London : O.U.P.

Guthrie, W.K.C. (1957) *In the Beginning*. London : Methuen

Haeckel, E. (1876) (trans. rev. Lankester) *The History of Creation*. London : King

Hale, M. (1677) *The Primitive Origination of Mankind*. London : Shrowsbery

Harris, V. (1966) *All Coherence Gone*. London : Cass

Hayek, F.A. (1955) *The Counter-Revolution of Science*. Glencoe : Free Press

Hepburn, R.W. (1955) George Hakewill : the virility of nature. *J.Hist. Ideas* 16, 135

Hesse, M.B. (1954) *Science and the Human Imagination.* London : S.C.M.

Hobbes, T. (1962) (ed. Oakesholt) *Leviathan.* New York : Collier

Holmes, O.W. (1968) (ed. Howe) *The Common Law.* London : Macmillan

Huntington, E. (1963) *The Human Habitat.* New York : Norton

Judson, S. (1968) Erosion rates near Rome, Italy. *Science* 160, 1444

Leach, E.R. (1961) Lévi-Strauss in the garden of Eden : an examination of some recent developments in the analysis of myth. *New York Academy of Sciences, Transactions*, 23, 386

Leach, E.R. (1966) The legitimacy of Solomon. Some structural aspects of Old Testament history. *Archiv. europ. sociol.* 7, 58

Lévi-Strauss, C. (1958) The structural study of myth. In (ed. Seboek) *Myth--A Symposium.* p.50 Bloomington : Indiana University Press

Lewis, C.S. (1964) *The Discarded Image.* London : C.U.P.

Locke, J. (1960) (ed. Laslett) *Two Treatises on Government.* London : C.U.P.

Lucretius (1951) (trans. Latham) *On the Nature of the Universe.* Harmondsworth : Penguin Books

Mac.Pherson, C.B. (1962) *The Political Theory of Possessive Individualism.* Oxford : Clarendon Press

Malthus, T.R. (1959) (foreword by Boulding) *Population : The First Essay.* Ann Arbor : University of Michigan Press

Manuel, F.E. (1962) The Prophets of Paris. Cambridge, Mass. : Harvard

Marsh, G.P. (1864) *Man and Nature.* New York : Scribner

Merrilees, D. (1968) Man the destroyer : late Quarternary changes in the Australian marsupial fauna. *J.Roy. Soc. West Austr.* 51, 1

Mill, J.S. (1961) *Auguste Comte and Positivism.* Ann Arbor : University of Michigan Press

Nasr, S.H. (1968) *The Encounter of Man and Nature.* London : Allen and Unwin

Nicolson, M.H. (1959) *Mountain Gloom and Mountain Glory.*
Ithaca : Cornell University Press

Niebuhr, R. (1945) *The Children of Light and the Children
of Darkness.* London : Nisbet

Northrop, F.S.C. (1946) *The Meeting of East and West.*
New York : Macmillan

Oldham, J.H. (1937) *The Oxford Conference-Official Report.*
New York : Willet Clark

Pawley, W.H. (1963) *Possibilities of Increasing World Food
Production.* Rome : Food and Agriculture Organisation of
the United Nations.

Piggott, S. (1965) *Ancient Europe ; A Survey.* Edinburgh :
Edinburgh University Press

Pius XI (1937) *Divina Redemptoris.* Washington : National
Catholic Welfare Conference

Redfield, R. (1953) *The Primitive World and its
Transformations.* Ithaca : Cornell University Press

Reicke, B. (1956) The knowledge hidden in the tree of
Paradise. *J.Semit. Studies* 1, 193

Renner, K. (1949) (ed. Kahn Freund) *The Institutions of
Private Law.* London : Routledge and Kegan Paul

Richardson, A. (1953) *Genesis 1–11. The Creation Stories and
the Modern World View.* London : S.C.M.

Ritchie, J. (1920) *The Influence of Man on Animal Life in
Scotland.* Cambridge : C.U.P.

Rousseau, J.J. (1953) (trans. Cohen) *The Confessions.*
Harmondsworth : Penguin Books

Scharzbaum, H. (1957) The overcrowded earth. *Numen* 4, 59

Schweitzer, A. (1923) (trans. Campion) *Civilization and Ethics.*
London : Black

Self, P. and H.J. Storing (1962) *The State and the Farmer.*
London : Allen and Unwin

Spengler, J.J. (1942) *French Predecessors of Malthus.*
Durham, N.C. : Duke University Press

Stow, J. (1890) (ed. Morley) *A Survey of London, Contayning
the Originall Antiquity, Increase, Moderne Estate, and
Description of that Citie, Written in the Year 1598.* London :
Routledge

Strangeland, C. E. (1904) *Pre-Malthusian Doctrines of Population.* New York : Columbia University Press

Szczesny, G. (1962) (trans. Garside) *The Future of Unbelief.* London : Heinemann

Tawney, R. H. (1938) *Religion and the Rise of Capitalism.* Harmondsworth : Penguin Books

Wagar, W. W. (1967). Modern views of the origins of the idea of progress. *J. Hist. Ideas* 28, 55

Wallace-Hadrill, D. S. (1968) *The Greek Patristic View of Nature.* Manchester : Manchester University Press

Watt, W. M. (1963) *Truth in the Religions.* Edinburgh : Edinburgh University Press

Watt, W. M. (1968) *Islamic Political Thought.* Edinburgh : Edinburgh University Press

Weber, M. (1930) (trans. Parsons) *The Protestant Ethic and the Spirit of Capitalism.* London, Allen and Unwin

White, L. (1962) *Medieval Technology and Social Change.* London : O.U.P.

Wynne-Edwards, V. C. (1962) *Animal Dispersion in relation to Social Behaviour.* Edinburgh : Oliver and Boyd

Index